# Out of My Mind

# Out of My Mind

## The Best of Joe Bayly

## Joseph T. Bayly

### Edited by Timothy Bayly

ZondervanPublishingHouse
*Grand Rapids, Michigan*

*A Division of HarperCollinsPublishers*

Out of My Mind
Copyright © 1993 by Mary Lou Bayly

Requests for information should be addressed to:
Zondervan Publishing House
Grand Rapids, Michigan 49530

**Library of Congress Cataloging in Publication Data**

Bayly, Joseph.
    Out of my mind : the best of Joe Bayly / Joseph T. Bayly ; edited by
Timothy Bayly.
       p.    cm.
    Includes bibliographical references and index.
    ISBN 0-310-60491-5
    1. Meditations. I. Bayly, Timothy, 1953–   . II. Title.
BV4832.2.B36  1993
242—dc20                                           93-24812
                                                      CIP

Unless otherwise marked, most Bible verses quoted in this book are the
author's paraphrase.

*Edited by Tim Bayly*
*Cover design by Cheryl Van Andel*
*Cover photo: © W. Cody/Westlight*

*Printed in the United States of America*

93 94 95 96 97 98 99 00 01 / DH / 10 9 8 7 6 5 4 3 2 1

# Contents

PART TWO
## OUT OF MY MIND: THE SEVENTIES

PART THREE
## OUT OF MY MIND: THE EIGHTIES

*To Mud,*
*wise and strong helpmate*
*for Dad*

# FOREWORD
## by Tim Bayly, editor

*. . . I kneel before the Father, from whom all fatherhood in heaven and on earth derives its name (Ephesians 3:14–15 NIV).*

Almost ten years ago I entered the pastoral ministry and began serving a yoked parish in rural Wisconsin. The churches were part of the denomination now known as the Presbyterian Church (USA), and from the beginning the challenges were large. A rather typical set of mainline problems characterized each congregation.

None of the parishioners knew anything about Dad, and although over the years Dad had been in a number of rural churches as part of his itinerant ministry, he was really not a man of the soil. Small-town/rural life was a bit mysterious to him. Being from Flushing, New York, he looked at communities like Pardeeville and Rosedale with a mixture of romanticism and discomfort.

He was my father, though, and from the beginning he and Mud (my mother's pet family name) put their shoulders to the plow with Mary Lee and me. When I was ordained in the Pardeeville sanctuary by John Knox Presbytery on October 23, 1983, Dad gave me the following charge:

> My beloved son, Timothy, I charge you as you enter upon your ministry:
>
> Have faith in God, who has called you. Seek to fulfill His expectations first of all, not those of His people, or your own. Build the church for His glory.
>
> Use the talents and training and gifts He has given you to the fullest, but don't depend on them. When your experience increases, don't depend on that. Depend on God

who has called you, to fulfill your calling. Depend on the Holy Spirit to work through you.

Do the work of an evangelist as one who himself has experienced deliverance and redemption. Carry the keys to the kingdom of heaven in your hand at all times. Be ready to give your time and life for one lost sheep as earnestly and diligently as you would for a thousand.

Tend the flock of God. Seek the lost ones, the defeated ones, the soul-sick ones, the wandering ones, and lovingly restore them. Then send them back into the battle.

Preach the Word of God, not avoiding those parts that are unpopular, or that cut across the grain of accepted opinion. Be prophetic, but exercise judgment upon yourself and your own actions first of all.

Respect authority, submit to authority, as to those appointed by God.

Be a careful counselor. Listen with your heart, guard the confidences you receive. Avoid and discourage gossip.

Pray for your people. When you work, you work; when you pray, God works. Never doubt that God can change people and situations, can resolve conflicts and bring peace where there has been trouble.

Love your people, care for them, have compassion on them. Encourage them to serve the Lord with joy and freedom. Share the Lord's work with them, train your lay persons to work in the fields of the Lord with you.

And enjoy your people. You are their servant, but you are also their friend. Share their lives, their joys as well as their sorrows, even as our Lord Jesus shared the lives of His disciples.

Be a responsible citizen in your community. Let your influence for ethics and morality be felt, always remembering that the community cannot be held to the standards of Christ's church.

Model love and care for your wife and children. Don't sacrifice them and your responsibility for them on the altar of your work and leadership in the church. Determine not to preach to others and see your own children castaways.

Guard your thoughts. Praise and worship God as a man, not just as a pastor. Don't covet another's position or possessions.

Enjoy God. Look for His fingerprints on every part of life. Cast your burdens on the Lord; don't bear them yourself. The battle is not yours, but God's. Find joy in the service, the place, the people God has given you.

Tonight you are being asked, "Wilt thou?" Some day you will be asked, "Hast thou?"

As an under-shepherd, serve the Great Shepherd so that you may answer in that day, "I have fought the good fight, I have finished my course, I have kept the faith."

Every couple of days during the first three years of ministry (until he died) Dad called on the phone to talk. Never one to be intrusive with his advice, still he was willing to help me with the tough decisions. He was a dependable friend and encourager.

At the end of my first year in the parish Dad and Mud read a selection of my sermons (I preached from manuscripts at the time) and gave me a written evaluation, not only on my preaching but also on the other areas of ministry. I doubt there was a more rigorous assessment of a pastor that year by any personnel committee! Since receiving those pages I've permanently kept them in the middle drawer of my desk and regularly reread them.

Nine years later it was time to move on. I received my second call in the Fall of 1991 and, leaving the Wisconsin dairy land, came to serve my present congregation in Bloomington, Indiana. Set just a couple of blocks off the campus of Indiana University, this parish is quite different from my first. I wish Dad were still here to help.

But I've been comforted in three ways.

First, I still have Mud. She learned many years ago to fill the gaps for her children left by her husband's absences, and she continues to be faithful to us, praying for us and giving us wise and godly counsel.

Second, the preparation of this volume has given me the opportunity to read through Dad's articles carefully. It's been much like talking with him on the phone. And if I've been encouraged and strengthened by hearing his voice again, I trust you will be too—assuming you're an old friend. And if this is your first reading of "Out of My Mind," welcome!

And third, on the eve of turning this manuscript in to Zondervan word came that Russ Hitt has gone to be with the Lord. He was the editor of *Eternity* for most of the years of "Out of My Mind," as well as one of Dad's close friends. Another father in the faith is gone. The cloud of witnesses is growing, but the strong arms linked with ours are disappearing and the day is evil.

It's hard to see these men leave us. But when Dad died six years ago and we were grieving his departure I was reminded that, however good my own father was, he was only a pale reflection of the perfections of our Heavenly Father. And whereas our earthly fathers have to leave us when they reach the end of their "three-score and ten" allotted years, we have the sure promise of Scripture that our Father in Heaven will never leave us or forsake us.

So when I miss Dad, I remind myself that God is The Father from Whom all fatherhood in heaven and earth gets its name. And I am comforted.

—Tim Bayly
Bloomington, Indiana
November 18, 1992

12

# JOE BAYLY
## by Chuck Swindoll

*For if the bugle produces an indistinct sound, who will prepare himself for battle?—1 Corinthians 14:8*

It was my distinct privilege to know Joe Bayly, not simply as an author but also as a man, a friend. Like many, many others, I had enjoyed the fruit of his pen for years, but it was not until we met that I began to understand why his words had touched me so deeply . . . why his bugle never produced an indistinct sound.

Over the years I observed that Joe's feelings, like his words, ran deep. He always listened well. He hated superficiality. He was authentic to the core. He enjoyed life but never at someone else's expense. When he wrote, he had the ability to say it straight, to keep it simple (even when dealing with profound subjects), and to make it live. Who can ever forget his description of the neighbor whose yard was covered with leaflets that fell from the "Gospel Blimp"? Who didn't understand the "gray slush" days of loneliness better after reading "A Psalm in a Hotel Room"? And who hasn't felt the lingering ache of grief when pondering the pages of *The View from a Hearse (The Last Thing We Talk About)*?

Joe's love for his wife and family was obvious to anyone who knew him. They remained a vital part of his powerful bugle call. They ranked high on his list of priorities, a rarity among most public figures, especially those as well-known as Joe. I always admired his remarkable ability to speak of his and Mary Lou's loss of three sons without manipulating self-pity. There was never any question, however, that those journeys through death's dark tunnels had taken a severe toll on both of them. No doubt it was the pain of those losses that nurtured within him such a tender, sensitive heart for God . . . and gave his bugle such a clarion call.

I loved the man's balance. He held to firm convictions and didn't hesitate to declare them, yet he remained tolerant and accepting of those who disagreed. He could be extremely serious, addressing life-and-death issues with keen logic, yet insert a needed touch of humor with wonderful ease. He knew what it meant to be busy, to meet deadlines, to handle the incessant demands of the publishing world, yet he thoroughly enjoyed relaxation. Most of all, I appreciated his skill in communicating both insightfully and creatively, yet without clichés. Whether it was poetry or fiction, a warning or an observation, a story with a twist or a plea for moral purity, Joe had a way of writing it with such freshness and aplomb, I simply could not lay his work aside with a shrug.

When the surprising news of Joe's death reached me, I truly grieved. To this day I find myself wishing he were still around, still calling me on the phone, still stabbing me awake with his penetrating ideas, still stretching me to think beyond predictable boundaries, still daring me to work hard, to write well, to win a hearing for the cause of Christ.

Alas, the old prophet ahead of his time is gone, but his literary bugle continues to produce a clear, distinct sound, preparing us for battle. How thankful I am that his writings survive him and thereby he, being dead, still speaks.

—Chuck Swindoll, Pastor
First Evangelical Free Church
of Fullerton (California)
October 20, 1992

# PREFACE: THE PERILS OF WRITING A COLUMN

This is a column of opinion. For the past seven years I have written it monthly for *Eternity* magazine.

What is a column of opinion? What is its function, what are the dangers of producing it or reading it?

Essentially, such a column is a look into the mind of the writer. It reflects his view of what's urgent or interesting.

The writer's perception of life, his perspective, controls the content of such a column. His presuppositions are the glasses through which he sees and judges reality. His contacts, experiences, relationships and reading are the climate and *cultus* of what he writes. Try as he may, he cannot escape his prejudices.

It was on the West Coast, after a meeting at which I had spoken, that I met a man who grasped this and gave me one of those warm compliments that are a writer's great reward.

"I told my wife I didn't want to miss tonight," the elderly man explained, as he shook my hand. "I've been reading your column in *Eternity* for quite a while, and so I already know you. But I wanted you to meet me."

A column is one-sided. It has no place for dialogue, although letters from readers and comments by those who are acquainted with the writer, or meet him, are most helpful in providing insights that he has missed or correctives to what he has written. (I think I have been most fortunate in having readers who respond to what I write.)

But by the time the reaction comes, the damage has been done. No correction can reach all readers.

The choice of what to write about is itself significant. What's important enough on the present horizon to claim the time of readers who will bother to listen? This is the writer's question.

"Important enough" is not quite right. When you get to know a person, even one who has the presumption to think that maybe he has something to say that you'd like to hear or need to hear, you soon tire of "Now hear this!" If you really get to know him, if he shows you his thinking in any sort of depth, you find humor and lightness along with opinions about weightier matters.

You also find that he has views on political, economic, and social—as well as religious—matters.

"Out of My Mind," along with everything else in this magazine, should be judged on the basis of its correspondence to the Bible, God's Word. This is the standard for all writing. This is the standard we have to set for ourselves, which doesn't mean that we can't be wrong. It rather indicates that our opinions, along with those of our readers, are subject to authority which can be invoked to prove us wrong. Or right.

What to write about? This is the columnist's recurring question as each deadline approaches.

—That Christian man who told me last week that he's read three books in the past twenty-five years, who's desperately concerned because of his teen-age daughter's rebellion?

—That medical doctor sitting next to me on the plane who told me about his son's dropping out after his freshman year in college, going to Haight-Ashbury, getting hooked on drugs, demanding a large sum of money? "But how can I pray for him, when I don't believe there is a God?" he asked me.

—That young couple who were commissioned at the church service last night for service with Wycliffe Bible Translators in New Guinea?

—That issue of the *Stanford Observer* that tells about the appointment of a new president of the university and the destruction of the retiring president's office by an arsonist (damage: $300,000), including books and personal possessions from nearly four decades in higher education? (The student body president announces a student referendum to determine whether the new president is acceptable or not. "The appointment . . . without the benefit of student participation or even student advice, represents a gross abuse by the Stanford trustees of the legal powers vested in them.")

—Or maybe the offer of a prize for selling twelve Bibles,

made by a Christian publishing house. The prize: "This handsome transistor radio."

Those are some of the live options at the moment. There will be others next month.

There's one other danger for a column writer: untimeliness. After I wrote last month's column on the policeman scattering the children at their Halloween play, we had the Democratic National Convention in Chicago. Few readers will think that the column wasn't some sort of comment on Mayor Daley's police action. But it wasn't—it was just an unfortunate incident of untimeliness.

Thanks for reading my column each month. I hope, somehow, that I'll get to know you too.

—Joe Bayly
November, 1968

# PART ONE

# OUT OF
# MY MIND:
# THE SIXTIES

*We would like to introduce you to Joseph T. Bayly and a new* Eternity *magazine column. One reading of one column will make you a permanent friend.*

—*ETERNITY*, OCTOBER 1961 ISSUE

# JOE BAYLY
## by C. Everett Koop

In the economy of God and in His sovereignty He puts certain people among us who will be up to the task He will place before them. Joe Bayly was such a man. He was my friend. He was the father of several of my patients. Three separate times I shared with him the bone-crushing grief when one of his children died. Indeed, as a surgeon I was involved in one way or another with each of these tragic deaths—deaths that to some people seemed as humanly unavoidable as they were tragic.

What was the real Joe Bayly like in the midst of drinking deeply from the cup of sorrow? He was like he always was— concerned for the spiritual welfare of others, available to go the extra mile for a friend (when it should have been the other way around), and apparently unflappable. Yet, entirely human.

No one could have lived through the sorrow of Joe Bayly's life with such equanimity without an abundant portion of the grace of God—which of course Joe acknowledged. But I said he was human.

Joe reminded me of Jesus praying in the twenty-sixth chapter of Matthew. God the Son talking with God the Father, and while mindful of His divine mission, nonetheless talking about the suffering to come in most human terms.

Joe wasn't a dishrag that said, "Thank you, Father," as each new blow was rained down upon him. He was human. He knew it was part of a sovereign plan of God but he hated it—naturally. After all, didn't Joe write *Psalms of My Life* and like the biblical psalmist run the gamut of emotion from wonder to sorrow to questioning to rebellion . . . finally to acceptance and praise? That was Joe.

Joe's eldest son always stood out from the crowd. When the boy wrote his essay for the National Merit Scholarship competition, it was about his faith in Christ. When he went to secular

21

college, his testimony was strong and clear, while his winsome personality and personal achievement attracted not only those who shared his faith but also those who didn't.

When he sustained a minor bump while sledding, his hemophilia allowed uncontrollable internal hemorrhage to threaten his life. When the young man lay dying in a suburban hospital near Philadelphia, Joe called me to ask that I see his son in consultation. It was too late.

For the third time in my career I told the same friend that his child was just a step away from heaven.

As I drove home from the hospital, I was terribly burdened, saddened by the apparent unfairness of it all. I was only the surgeon; Joe was the father. What unspeakable thoughts must have been going through his mind. And yet as I left him at the hospital elevator, he was apparently stoic, certainly resigned, at once a figure most pitiable, but among his son's attendants a tower of strength. That was Joe Bayly. No wonder he was the source of so much sage advice to the countless young people who sought his counsel over the years.

The memorial service for that boy in the Blue Church in Delaware County, Pennsylvania, was the most heart-wrenching, yet triumphant, hour I can remember. The church was packed not only with Joe's friends, but also with all the new friends his son had made at college. These young people felt inexplicably deprived of a truly unique person to whom they had become unusually attached, but whose special view of life—and death—they could not understand.

After few preliminaries, Joe Bayly went to the front of the church. The lump in my throat was so large I could barely swallow. The lump in Joe's throat was so large he could barely talk. But he did, and his opening words are burned forever in my mind: "I want to speak to you tonight about my earthly son and his Heavenly Father . . ."

Joe poured out his heart. Tears streamed down the faces of almost everyone present. That night, the message Joe brought to his son's college friends started a large number of them down a path in search of what Joe and his son had—and many of them found it in faith in Jesus Christ. That was Joe Bayly.

—C. Everett Koop, M.D.
October, 1991

# Christian Incendiarism

## October 1961

Bear Lake is a flag-stop on the Erie Railroad in western Pennsylvania. Once it was a thriving lumber town, but when the state highway was put through, Bear Lake was by-passed. Today nobody is employed locally, and community spirit is almost non-existent.

A few years ago Burkett Smith came to Bear Lake Evangelical United Brethren Church. It was his first pastorate, and he hadn't yet learned to accept the status quo.

Smith soon discovered that the church members had little concern for their neighbors, or for the community affairs.

The new pastor was invited to serve as an honorary member of the Bear Lake Volunteer Fire Department, and he accepted. Later Smith found that not one of his church men was in the fire company.

When the next men's meeting of the church rolled around, Burkett Smith told the fellows that they ought to be active in community affairs. For instance, why weren't any of them members of the volunteer fire department?

The young pastor's words made sense to at least five of the men. Next time the fire company met, these five from the church were present for their first meeting.

The following Sunday morning, just as the service was about to begin at the Bear Lake E.U.B. Church, five men from the fire department walked in—men who hadn't previously attended the church. They came in single file and went straight down to the front row. That Sunday Burkett Smith preached on the Christian responsibility of parents.

Next Sunday the five were back at church—this time with

their families. And within the next few months, all five of the firemen became Christians, together with their wives.

*   *   *

Søren Kierkegaard, mid-nineteenth-century critic of the Danish church, had his own opinions about Christians and fire fighting.

One of his polemic essays, published in a Copenhagen newspaper, answered the question, "Would it not be best now to stop ringing the fire alarm?"

"Strictly speaking," wrote Kierkegaard, "it is not I who am ringing the fire bell; it is I who am starting the fire. . . . For according to the New Testament, Christianity is incendiarism. Christ Himself says, 'I am come to set fire on the earth, and it is already burning' [Luke 12:49]."*

*   *   *

Why did Kierkegaard choose a Copenhagen newspaper (*The Fatherland*), a political one at that, as a vehicle for so much of his writing? Because he felt that sermons should not be preached in churches, but in the streets.

"It harms Christianity in a high degree and alters its very nature, that it is brought into an artistic remoteness from reality, instead of being heard in the midst of real life, and that precisely for the sake of the conflict. For all this talk about quiet places and quiet hours, as the right element for Christianity, is absurd."†

And so Kierkegaard chose to preach his sermons in a secular newspaper, finding such a medium the closest approximation to preaching in the streets. Thus he attained his goal of confronting various interests with the thought of Christianity.

---

*Søren Kierkegaard, *Attack Upon Christendom* tr. by Walter Lowrie (Princeton University Press, 1944).
†Ibid.

It was through George Whitefield that John Wesley was converted to preaching outside the church. For a long time Wesley was opposed to Whitefield's "fields preaching," until one day he agreed to give it a try. "All my life I've been so careful to do everything decently and in order. Why, I must confess that I almost consider the saving of souls a sin if it isn't done in a church."

As the two men approached the little hill outside Bristol that Sunday afternoon, Wesley commented, "I submit myself to be considered vile."

But then Wesley saw the large group of people, about three thousand, waiting silently for spiritual food. And he began to preach, "The Spirit of the Lord is upon me, because he hath anointed me to preach the gospel to the poor" (Luke: 4:18).

That was the beginning of concentration upon England's great unchurched masses, as tens of thousands heard the gospel in fields and prisons, mines and factories. And the poor and the oppressed received the Lord Jesus Christ.

If the Spirit of the Lord is upon us, He may take us out of our own comfortably established churches into fields and newspapers and firehouses.

# *What Do the Jews Remember?*

**December 1961**

What do the Jews remember?

A trench two blocks long, twelve feet wide, six feet deep, "filled to overflowing with bodies of women, children, old men, boys and girls in their teens ... frozen pools of blood ...

children's caps, toys, ribbons, baby bottles and rubber pants . . . torn off hands and feet . . . everything spattered with blood and brains."*

Another time, another place. Here a great mound of earth, several hundred feet long, more than six feet high—"a good shooting range." Several trucks packed with people, other people of all ages undressing, piling their clothes and shoes in neat bundles . . . guards with whips . . . the sound of shooting behind the earthworks.

"The mothers undressed little children without screaming or weeping. . . . They stood around in little family groups, kissed each other, said farewells, and waited. I watched a family of about eight persons, a man and woman about fifty, with their grown up children. . . . An old woman with snow-white hair was holding a little baby in her arms, singing to it and tickling it. The baby was cooing with delight . . ."

And then the SS man on the other side of the mound shouted, and the next batch of people—including the family of eight—was led through an opening and down into a pit nine feet deep. There, lying naked on top of other naked Jews dead and dying, they were shot in the back of the neck.*

\*     \*     \*

Soon after the end of World War II, I was in Europe for a Christian students' camp. In the cabin for which I was responsible were six or seven German students, all of whom had served in Hitler's army.

Several of these young Germans had come from Christian homes. One night we were talking about the war, and they told of refusing to take dancing lessons because their parents had taught them that dancing was wrong. This decision had meant sacrifice, they said, since social dancing was required of officer candidates and they had thus missed out on promotion.

---

*\*Trial of the Major War Criminals,* vol. 7, quoted by Malcolm Hay, *Europe and the Jews* (Beacon Press, 1950), from a Russian officer's testimony.
\*Ibid., from the evidence of a German witness.

I remember my feeling of surprise. Christians were the same everywhere—they weren't afraid to speak out, even against Hitler, when it came to social dancing.

\* \* \*

During the trial of Adolph Eichmann, the *Jerusalem Post Weekly* reported a courtroom clash between counsel Dr. Robert Servatius and prosecution witness Dr. Salo Baron, Jewish historian at Columbia University.

"The theme of this debate could be summed up as predestination versus moral choice. Dr. Servatius's questions and answers posed the problem: How can you blame a man who is swept forward by the onrushing tide of history? This is destiny. The end result of the Nazi extermination program was not the liquidation of Jewry, but its revival in a free and flourishing state. Why punish a man who was only an instrument of this historical destiny?

"Dr. Baron answered that each man has a moral responsibility to himself, to mankind and to God, and even the most fervent Christian believers in predestination believed firmly that criminals should be punished on this earth. It was the duty of each man [in the Nazi state] to look into his heart and decide that he could break away from the madness which enveloped a hysterical and insane mass movement."

# *What Would Happen If ...*

## July 1962

If a preacher should arise and say that our biggest problem is not Russian Communism, but the sins of the American people of God, the corruption of our own nation;

. . . and call his own people dishonest, unjust, full of adultery, covetous, liars, oppressors of the helpless;

. . . and say that free-born Americans have sunk to the level of beasts, behaving like well-fed stallions in our lust;

. . . scorn our high standard of living, condemn our love of luxury, and pronounce God's judgment upon us for exploiting minority groups and the poor;

—And when he spoke of the future

would say that there is no hope of ever returning to the halcyon days of the Coolidge administration,

. . . nor of creating a bright new order by liberal social reform;

. . . that a conservative President—or a liberal Congress— wouldn't make a bit of difference,

. . . nor could economic justice be restored by repealing the income tax, or bringing the labor movement under the anti-trust laws,

. . . or by repealing the poll tax, or passing social legislation that would cover everybody from the cradle to the grave;

But the only hope

is a coming King

. . . not of the U.S.A., but of a better country;

And meanwhile

we had better get ready for some bad times—

. . . because it won't be long before the Russians overcome us

—not just overtake us, but overcome us, take vast numbers of our American people into captivity, to Siberia and Hungary and China;

. . . and our alliances with England and France and Germany will not help us in that day,

. . . nor our bases in Spain and Turkey, our nuclear arms and roving submarines,

. . . because God is going to do this, God is going to help the godless Russian Communists defeat America, Citadel of Freedom:

What would happen?

WOULD THAT PREACHER
win a Freedoms Foundation award,
... would people flock to hear him,
... would they pay for full-page ads to carry his words in the
daily papers,
... time on the radio and TV;
Or would they
cut up his speech in Congress,
... burn it in the Governor's mansion,
... threaten his life in Anathothburg, his home town,
... put him in prison?

I THINK WE KNOW THE ANSWERS.

... and if we don't, Jeremiah could tell us.

# Is Every New Bible Version a Blessing?

## October 1962

When the Revised Standard Version was completed in 1952, a call to arms resounded throughout Fundamentalism. A new test of orthodoxy was forthwith introduced: continued use of the King James Bible.

Copies of the new translation were burned in pulpits. Granted, such instances were few and far between. But even fewer were the critics within Fundamentalism of such blasphemy.

Doubtless the objectors had their grounds. Hebrew and Greek scholars are not generally best qualified to communicate in modern written English. (Prime example: the Berkeley Version.) A case could be made for the inclusion of skilled writers, of the same professional caliber as the Greek and Hebrew scholars, on every translation team. Surely writers, as well as translators, are God's gift to the Church.

But on the other hand, a skilled writer is not a translator. Many people received enlightenment from the freshness of J. B. Phillips' paraphrases (especially *Letters to Young Churches,* his first and best). But why do author and publisher now call this a "translation"?

For a few years after the Revised Standard Version was shot down in flames, no Bible in modern English existed to satisfy any desire these people might have for something fresh. And so demand built up behind the dam erected by Fundamentalism's leaders. Some Christians did not want the King James replaced in the pulpit, but personal Bible reading was another matter.

And so, when new translations and paraphrases appeared, demand rushed through the dam's floodgates. Williams (republished), Verkuyl—Berkeley, Phillips, Amplified Bible, New English Bible: each appeared in turn and was either accepted acritically by Fundamentalism's arbiters, or was subjected to criticism mild by Revised Standard criteria.

The Revised Standard Version may be superior to the New English Bible on doctrinal and literary grounds (the latter especially for American readers), but it would be hopeless to attempt to prove this to a segment of the Bible-reading public. The Revised Standard Version may be a model of literal translation beside the Phillips paraphrase, but a generation's mind has been molded to exclude the one and admit the other.

Conservative Christian scholars, both biblical and literary, may privately bewail the widespread acceptance and influence of a certain version. But outside the classroom their mouths and pens are silent—probably because this version has grown within the matrix of fundamental authorship and publication. These people are our team—they're Bible-believing Christians—so we automatically accept what they produce. And besides, people are getting a blessing from it.

The most recent addition to the list is *The Teen-Age Version of the Holy Bible.* The Preface states that "Teenagers themselves have been the judges of what they want, need, and will use." "Easy-to-understand language" has replaced big words. Reason: "Surely there is little excuse for a translator to force his reader to be constantly translating further as he reads."

Now this version is doctrinally sound. The "translator" is a man who loves the Lord. The Holy Spirit will use this Bible—even as He uses the Revised Standard Version—for spiritual enlightenment.

But where are we headed? Will a new version be issued for the gifted child?

And where are we headed when those who stand for verbal inspiration are the very ones who are opening the floodgates to novel, gadgetry ideas in Bible production? Does it matter that a Bible for teenagers says that God created "the heaven and the earth" (Gen. 1:1) instead of "the heavens and the earth"? What would we have said if the Revised Standard translators had changed this? Or is "virgin" the only word of Scripture worthy of serious defense? And what about changing our Lord's imperative, "Be ye therefore perfect, even as your Father which is in heaven is perfect" (Matt. 5:48), into a simple future, "Therefore, you shall be perfect . . ."

We must be more critical of such translations, not less critical. Those who believe in verbal inspiration and add to or subtract from the Scriptures are worthy of greater censure than those who take a different position on inspiration. Scholarship is as necessary for the conservative as for the liberal. And beauty is a thing to be desired in any attempt to bring forth the Word of God afresh.

# Lord, Raise Up a Negro Prophet
**November 1962**

For a number of years, speaking, writing, and editing, I have espoused the cause of Negroes. I have not merely accepted, but have been thankful for court decisions in the area of equal civil rights for Negroes. I have repeatedly told my white Christian friends, including those who live in the South, that God will judge us if we are content to enjoy advantages at the expense of others, and the sooner the situation is changed, the better.

Now I have something to say to my Negro Christian friends, something that is seldom said today by thinking white people, especially thinking church people, because we may so easily be accused of speaking without love. Or we may seem to lack understanding of the basic problems confronting Negroes in contemporary culture. Or what is worse, we may seem to be using this as a lever to maintain the status quo, which is so unbalanced in our favor. I run these risks in what I say.

Negro crime and immorality constitute one of the gravest problems in American society today. Whenever I speak at correctional institutions, I am struck by the disproportionate number of Negroes—men, women, boys, girls. I immediately rationalize this situation to myself: If you had been forced to live in the sort of environment these people have always known, if you had always found discrimination based upon color of skin, you yourself would probably have gotten into trouble, your own children might be in this group of young people before you.

A Philadelphia newspaper tells of a public school—located in a Negro neighborhood—in which 70 percent of the children have been of illegitimate parentage. I read in those same newspapers about Negro gangs, about narcotics peddling and numbers gambling among Negroes.

Perhaps the trigger for what I write was the thirteen-year-old child whom a medical friend of mine assisted in a difficult delivery a couple of Sundays ago. Or it may have been the young Negro woman converted in a university, who said, "I just can't face life as a married woman among my people. The standard is too low, at least in the city where I live . . . I'd rather remain single."

Now I am aware of the cultural displacement of the Negro masses who emigrate to our Northern cities, week after week. I know something about—nothing of—the poverty, the crowded housing, the discrimination. It is easy for me to sympathize with Negroes and rationalize Negro crime and immorality.

But there is one thing I can't rationalize. That is the almost complete silence of Negro leaders, including church leaders, about the situation. I have listened for a prophet's voice raised against these evils, but heard none. I have only heard the multiplied voices of judges raised against the evils of white discrimination.

It is morally unhealthy to sit in judgment upon another race, another people, another person, demanding and receiving confessions of guilt and sin, meanwhile remaining silent about one's own sin. The sin of discrimination is a heavy weight upon the white Christian conscience, both North and South; the sin of sexual immorality and crime seems to lie light upon the Negro conscience.

Perhaps if I were closer to the heart of Negro affairs, I would hear voices raised. I hope so. Yet I wonder if this is so, since newspapers that report the demands of Negro leaders for Negroes to be appointed to high administrative posts in public education and government would almost certainly report demands of these same leaders for a Christian standard of morality among their own people.

Not that I consider white America moral. I don't, and I can't rationalize the situation. But I hear Christian voices raised, I read articles warning of impending judgment.

I know that social change is accomplished one step at a time. I know, too, that God delivered His people from Egypt before He gave the Divine Law. But today we are not in the darkness of pre-Revelation. We have the Light of our Lord Jesus Christ. And

Christian morality has never, to my knowledge, waited for social betterment. Those slaves (white) on the Island of Crete, about whom St. Paul wrote to Titus, were expected to influence their masters by their personal morality (Titus 2:9–10)—not by their demands for equality. And I sense that a significant decrease in the number of Negro births out of wedlock, in the number of unwed Negro mothers on the relief rolls, in the number of Negro youths embroiled in delinquency, a significant improvement in Negro morality would do more to change the climate of white opinion toward Negroes than all the pressure groups can ever achieve.

So, I look for a prophet, a Negro prophet, who will scorn personal advantage, who will warn his people of sin and judgment, and preach Jesus Christ according to the Scriptures. God give us a thousand such men.

Meanwhile I shall continue to speak out to exercise my slight influence on behalf of the Christian and American attitude toward equal rights for Negroes. But as we descend the ladder of white privilege, I hope we meet others ascending up the ladder of Negro morality.

# Pastors in the Modern World
**December 1962**

A few weeks ago, when we started our classes in psychiatry," a medical student told me, "the professor said that even if we don't specialize in the field, we'll still have an awful lot of people come to us with their problems, wanting help.

" 'But don't get proud when that happens,' this professor said. 'In a previous generation they'd have gone to their minister. It's their loss of confidence in the ministry that makes these people come to the doctor today for counseling.' "

If the psychiatrist was correct in his diagnosis (and I believe he was), why have so many people today lost confidence in their ministers? How has the situation changed from earlier years? And can anything be done about it?

Here are some of my suggestions, based upon observation and a brief recent exposure to the problem of the pastorate.

(1) The ministry today is staggering under an ever-increasing weight of organization, meetings, activities. It's hard for a minister to keep his head above water, let alone do an effective work of preaching and counseling.

Of course, the ministry isn't the only part of modern life to be confronted with the problems of increasing complexity and organization. Doctors, for example, have resisted pressures that might have removed them from their primary work of healing by turning administration of their hospitals and organization of their business affairs over to professionals trained in these fields rather than in medicine. And it seems to me that the ministry must adopt the same policy, for which ample New Testament precedent is found in Acts 6:2–7.

Dr. Harold Englund tells of his first meeting with the consistory of a church in Midland, Michigan, to which he had just gone as a minister.

They had two things to say to the new pastor. "First, we want you to be a good example to the people in our church, and that means you won't be out every night of the week, away from home. And second, we don't want you to do anything in the church here that we can do." Dr. Englund says that the willingness of men in that church to assume all sorts of responsibilities freed him for a spiritual ministry.

We mustn't be content to be "Jack-of-all-trades" ministers, but must recapture the New Testament and Reformation principle of the universal priesthood of believers. Surely the Spirit of God has His gifted men even in the smaller congregations, but they must be sought out and trained.

(2) Ministers today are too busy for their own good, and for the good of their wives and children and the good of their people.

Nothing discourages counseling and personal relations more effectively than an "I can only spare a minute, make it brief" kind of attitude. Few of us would say this, but we give the impression nonetheless.

A minister friend of mine was concerned when two of his three sons began to stutter. He made an appointment for them to see a speech therapist (who was also a psychologist), and later had a conference himself.

"That psychologist literally cursed me," the minister said. "He told me I was responsible for that speech defect, and that I was ruining my boys' lives.

"'When did you last take your family on a vacation?' he asked me.

"Well, it had been a long, long time. I was too busy to take time with my family. I remember I used to say that the Devil never takes a vacation, so why should I?—And I never stopped to think that the Devil wasn't to be my example.

"I went out of that man's office, got a camping trailer, and in a few days we were headed West. The second day out my wife nudged me, and I listened to the conversation in the back seat. There wasn't a trace of a speech defect from those boys. I pulled over to the side of the road and bawled like a baby."

Ministers will always be busy men, but we must have rest: inward rest and times of refreshing.

And in the midst of our busy lives, we must impress our young people, our sick, our depressed, our invalids, our busy executives with our personal availability—more than that, our desire to give hours of time to their needs and problems.

(3) Ministers today must establish priorities in their work. Our time must be disciplined, the more so because we have no rigid 9 to 5 schedule. Some ministers spend too much time helping their wives with housework.

We must also have ideological priorities, and refuse to be diverted from the biblical essentials of our preaching-counseling ministry. We must not be small men who "major in the minors."

(4) In larger churches, personal counseling is often delegated to the younger minister—just out of seminary—while the older minister, with the maturity and wisdom of experience, limits his work to preaching and organizing. Such an arrangement

legislates against the minister's understanding of his people and consequent effectiveness in his preaching, as well as against a strong counseling ministry. We cannot become really acquainted with our people in meetings, nor at their weddings and funerals.

(5) The lack of personal contact with people in their joys and sorrows and ordinary life results in a theoretical type of preaching, unrelated to the kitchen and shop, the high school and courtroom. The modern minister must be at home in the supermarket, machine shop, the homes of his people, if he is to preach Christ with power. Preaching is strongest when it reaches as high as God and as low as the people. Today we are likely to gain mere middle altitude.

(6) Ministers haven't always kept their mouths shut, and this is necessary for effective counseling. Doctors, on the whole, are much more generally respected for observing professional ethics, especially in preserving inviolate confidential information, than are ministers. Public opinion of the ministry is no higher than the standards we set and maintain.

(7) Ministers have tended to lose contact with the poor, with those who consider themselves ill-used by life and their fellows. We shall continue to fail in our ministry to all classes and groups as long as we insist upon raising walls of political, social and economic convictions held with fervor approaching that with which we hold biblical doctrine. The Apostle Paul's principle of being "all things to all men" (1 Cor. 9:22) that we may win some to Christ is true and necessary today.

In a previous period of Church history, when the Church was affluent and its ministers increased with goods, a minority who wanted to break through to God and their fellows took a vow of poverty. Perhaps we should rethink our standard of living today, our houses and cars, and ask whether it may be God's will for us to choose a lower level for the sake of communicating the gospel to all men in our day. According to Philippians 2, the *Kenosis* of Christ has personal implications for us.

(8) The minister today must have a compelling sense of purpose. We must work individually and corporately with the same sort of drive shown by the team that is orbiting astronauts

around the earth. Our calling is the most important one that men can answer.

V. I. Lenin is described by a biographer in these terms: Lenin was a man wholly devoid of personal ambition; he possessed a supreme ability to work with various types of men; he had utter devotion to the communist cause; he had singleness of mind; he had a sense of the movement of mind in ordinary people; and he had a great ability to blend theory and practice into coherent and decisive policy.

God, make us such men for Thee, flames of fire for Thine eternal kingdom.

# *The Fine Print of a Year*

## January 1963

A year of minor incidents and impressions has ended—insignificant in the face of great movements of nations and human affairs, but important to the little me (and you) who experienced them. And we are sure that they're important to our Heavenly Father, who not only sent Roman legions marching, but also saw a tiny sparrow fall to the ground.

Some impressions stand out because we wrote them down; others need no mechanical aid to remembrance, but only wait the flash of association—a day, a time of year, a fragrance, a falling leaf, a baby's cry—to emerge into our consciousness.

Here are some of my minor impressions of 1962 in retrospect.

*Saturday, January 27.* This afternoon we took the older children ice-skating. On our way we passed St. George's Episcopal Church.

"Why do so many Episcopal churches have red doors?"

"I don't know."

"When they first started painting them red, they wanted to show that entrance into the Church is through the blood of Jesus Christ."

*Friday, March 30.* Packed some books for mailing this morning.

Lord, this cardboard box—see, it says, "Bursting limit 200 pounds per square inch." The box maker knew how much strain the box would take, what weight would crush it.

Thou art wiser than the box maker, Maker of my spirit, my mind, my body.

Does the box know when the pressure increases close to the limit? No, it knows not. But I know when the breaking point is near. And so I pray, Maker of my soul, Determiner of the pressures piled upon me, call a halt, lest I be broken.

Or else change the pressure rating of this fragile container of Thy grace, so that I may bear more. Amen.

*Tuesday, April 3.* A letter came today from my friend Norton Sterrett, missionary to India's students. He discussed the biblical teaching about confession of sin to other Christians (James 5:16)—a phenomenon of the Ruanda revival and other lesser known works of God in recent times. Is it God's will for us to tell about our sins and failures, if the other person hasn't been involved? (There is too little of this give-and-take type of correspondence between Christians today, in my opinion.)

*Wednesday, May 9.* Checked out a hundred-year-old book from the library today, *Mothers of England,* which contained advice on child-training. One sentence: "If you punish a child with the same severity for breaking something as you do for telling a lie, you are implying that immorality is no more serious than awkwardness."

*Sunday, June 5.* In his morning message, Pastor Cressy mentioned the occasional pastoral call when you're met at the door by the lady who says, with a mixture of apology and exasperation, "This has been one of those days!"

"You know what that means," the pastor explained. "It means that you're part of it."

I had a pastoral visit last week with an older lady who lives alone. She had just moved into a new apartment—modest, because she has very little treasure on earth. There was no apology for how things looked, although they were still upset from moving.

As we talked about God's faithfulness in the midst of her considerable problems, she drew a piece of lined paper out of her Bible.

"Would you like to read this?" she asked, almost shyly. "It's something I wrote down one night when I couldn't sleep. This is my desire for the years that remain."

I read it, and I was moved. Here is what was written on the paper:

> *Oh that I might die to self and every world ambition;*
> *Oh that I might yielded be under every condition;*
> *Oh that I might constantly pray in the Holy Spirit;*
> *Thy commandments plainly hear,*
> *And instantly obey them when I hear them.*
> *"Blessed be ye poor, for yours is the kingdom of God."**

*Saturday, July 28.* Rode the merry-go-round tonight with happy David and worried Nathan, while Mary Lou looked on and waved each time we passed. Timmy kept up with us, running, for three times around.

"Every good gift and every perfect gift is from above, and cometh down from the Father of lights" (James 1:17).

*Tuesday, August 7.* Saw a magnificent display of northern lights after the evening meeting at Inter-Varsity's training camp for students in Northern Michigan, Cedar Campus.

*Sunday, September 2.* Spoke at an institution for delinquent girls this afternoon. One girl in her early teens told me afterward, "I'm so glad I was sent here, because it was here that I found Jesus."

*Wednesday, October 10.* This morning I spoke to children in the middle grades of Delaware County Christian School at their weekly chapel service. Tonight, just before he went to bed,

---

*Luke 6:20.

Timmy remembered to give me a batch of letters written by his fourth-grade class to thank me for coming—a sort of subliminal exercise in English and writing.

One letter stood out.

Dear Mr. Bayly:
> Thank you for speaking to us today. I learned that I had been proud. I had never really noticed it because it came natural to me.

Love, Phil Mell

"Verily I say unto you, Whosoever shall not receive the kingdom of God as a little child shall in no wise enter therein."*

*Monday, November 5.* The morning mail brought a letter the *New Yorker* might have printed under its heading, "Letters we never finished reading."

Here's how it began:

AIRLINES CLERGY BUREAU
Municipal Airport—Sacramento, Calif.

TO ALL MINISTERS:
> Greetings in the Name of our Lord.
> I have fought a good fight, I have finished my course, I have kept the Faith, henceforth there is laid up for YOU a reduced rate on airlines, Hotels, Motels, and Car Rentals . . .

My reaction was mixed, but I guess the predominant feeling was, "Poor guy, he's so ignorant of spiritual matters."

Lord, keep us who aren't ignorant from offending Thee by any lightness in handling Thine Eternal Word. And guard us against the temptation to use spiritual means to achieve material ends. Amen.

---

*Today Phil Mell is a loving Christian husband and father with a personality marked, chiefly, by humility.

# *Beauty Out of Cinders*

## April 1963

Have you ever held a cluster of trailing arbutus in your cupped hands and buried your nose in its delicate pink and white flowers?

If you have, you'll agree with me that this is one of God's best fragrances—a sufficient reason, all by itself, for the creation of noses.

I've only seen this flower three times, yet every spring I think of it. That's because of the first time, when I was six or seven years old. We lived in the mountains of Central Pennsylvania; my father traveled a great deal on the railroad.

One night in the spring, just as the moon was coming up over Pleasant Valley, he came home with a bulky but light package, loosely wrapped in newspaper, in his arms.

"Mary, I brought you something," he said. "It was growing in some cinders by the railroad tracks." He probably said where the tracks were, some little town—perhaps Cresson—where he'd been that day.

"Open it up."

We children shoved close. Suddenly the room was filled with the fragrance of those lovely flowers as the newspaper fell apart.

That night I knew that trailing arbutus was the most beautiful flower in the world. And I knew that my father loved my mother.

\* \* \*

"Every period in life has its special problem, and even a newborn baby has a lesson to learn—to receive and give love. But this problem really began before his birth. It began with you two, his parents. Unless you love each other, you cannot properly love him nor provide a love-warmed home for him. . . . True, there is no guarantee that your children will grow up healthy and happy just because you two are in love with each other. You must also have the knowledge and the will to raise them right.

"One thing is certain, however, the children of parents who do not love each other have a sad time of it. Their home is a spawning ground for mental and moral ills.

"No study of what every child needs, therefore, can do better than dwell hard and long on the question of how parents can so replenish each other's affections, can so fulfill each other's need of love, that in its mutual overflow there will be more than enough to envelop the children with warmth and comfort. . . ."*

Several weeks ago I participated in a student conference sponsored by Inter-Varsity Christian Fellowship. Students from out of town were placed in Christian homes.

Toward the end of the three days, in a "sharing" session, a young woman said that she had been a Christian for only two years and had never been in a Christian home before. "I've sometimes wondered if there were such a thing as a Christian home, and what it would be like. My own mother and father aren't Christians, or even religious. Well, now I know—and I could just rave about the home where I've been staying here at this conference. It's going to make a difference in my entire outlook on marriage and having children.

"This family where I'm staying has eight children. They live in a big old house. Their furniture is old and sort of put together—but lovingly put together. There are separate boys' and girls' bathrooms, like at school. There's a big dining table—the father's at one end, the mother's at the other.

"The mother's so peaceful; you'd never know she has eight children."

---

*David Goodman, *A Parents' Guide to the Emotional Needs of Children* (New York: Hawthorn Books, 1959).

Betty Scott Stam, C.I.M. missionary killed by Chinese Communists in 1934, wrote to her parents when she was a student at Moody Bible Institute: "Because you loved, I am."

Whether she meant any more than the mere creation of life—which may be accomplished without love—or not, her statement has lengthening implications during the life of a child and teenager.

How many children, even in Christian homes, can say the other truth: "Because you didn't love, I am not . . . secure . . . trusting Jesus Christ . . . walking in His ways."

\* \* \*

White is not the mere absence of black; it is the presence of all the colors of the spectrum.

And Christian perfection is not the mere absence of sin; it is the presence of all the beauty of God's holy, loving character.

\* \* \*

Arbutus from cinders, beauty from ashes, tender love from a marriage that may be falling to pieces: thus does God work . . . when we turn to Him in faith.

# Hush, Hush about Morality

Where Do We Take Our Stand? or Salt Losing Its Savor

**June 1963**

This year, speaking to college students—especially in dormitory and fraternity discussions—I've been asked

45

one question again and again. It almost always takes this form: "Why is premarital intercourse wrong?"

Often there are explanatory or qualifying clauses: "—with the girl you're going to marry some day"; "—when it seems to work out well in parts of Europe where it's pretty commonly accepted"; "—if neither of you sees anything wrong with it"; "—since he may be shipped overseas any minute"; "—when it seems, like the psych professor says, to be merely a normal response to a human appetite."

Those clauses reveal the more basic question, one that is foundational to the Christian religion: Are there such things as moral absolutes, or is everything relative, subject to the conditions of time and place and opinion? The latter view, probably held (consciously or unconsciously) by a majority on today's academic scene, was expressed by the scientist Sir Julian Huxley in a recent issue of *Nature* magazine: "In adapting our old educational system to our new vision, much cargo will have to be jettisoned—once-noble but now moldering myths, shiny but useless aphorisms, Utopian but unfounded speculations, nasty projections of our prejudices and repression. . . . Children are not born with a load of original sin derived from a 'Fall.'. . . There are no Absolutes of Truth or Virtue."

Now I believe in academic freedom of expression, but I find it hard to understand why a scientific magazine should lend itself to an attack upon the Judeo-Christian religion. Even harder for me to understand is the silence of qualified and respected scientists who are Christians, in the face of such an attack. Why, in scientific publications or in classrooms, is there so seldom a rebuttal of such opinions? The failure of Christians in Academe to avail themselves of the prerogatives of academic freedom may go far toward explaining why the historic Christian faith is no longer a live option to the educated person. "The children of this world are in their generation wiser than the children of light" (Luke 16:8).

But the general silence among Christians about moral absolutes today, both in and out of the university community, is disturbing—like the small lump, alarming out of proportion to its size, to one who fears a malignant tumor. This vague disturbance was expressed several years ago by an editorialist in *Christianity and Crisis:*

> For about a generation now there has been a growing tendency among Christian intellectuals to eschew and condemn moralism. . . . One of the things which attracted the ancient Romans to Christianity was the rigorous Christian morality, especially regarding sex, and the self-discipline of the Christian home. Doubtless many of the intellectuals of the Roman world branded these simple Christians as being too simple and too moralistic. I suspect that if Jesus, or Paul, or one of the early Church fathers were to preach in America today, many Christian intellectuals would accuse them of the same. I do not know for sure. That is what disturbs me. But at the risk of being a superficial moralist I raise these questions: Have Christians sold too many hostages to the modern vogue of relativism? And where do we take our stand, particularly on the matters of sex and the preservation of the Christian home?

Where do we take our stand?

On the ground of moral absolutes: as a convinced Christian I have no other answer. Jesus Christ and Paul and Moses and Elijah have determined our position. When the Christian Church yields to relativism, the salt loses its savor, the world loses its light (Matt. 5:13, 14).

Our temptation, especially with the unconverted, is to bypass the absolute demands of a Holy God, ineffably pure, and "just preach the gospel." For we know that men cannot achieve moral purity and legal justification before coming to Christ.

But there's a difference between saying, "Come to Jesus just as you are. Don't wait until you're better," and saying, "It doesn't matter what God is like, what His standards are."

God dealt with His people, in the childhood of the race, by revealing absolute moral law. Jesus Christ began His ministry of introducing the Kingdom by confirming the law and defining God's ultimate standards. St. Paul said that in his personal experience, sin, by the commandments of the law, became exceedingly sinful (Rom. 7:13).

Should we deal with our generation otherwise? Is not the present uncertainty about moral absolutes (including premarital intercourse) one result of introducing boys and girls, men and women, to grace without prior exposure to law? We hedge on the demands of absolute law at the risk of undermining absolute grace; when we lighten law we cheapen grace.

In a fraternity lounge or on the sand at Fort Lauderdale, we must not bypass the moral absolutes that include our hearers under the judgment of God. To do so is not merely to cast our pearls before swine (Matt. 7:6); it is to gain an audience and lose our mission.

# Cleaning Out My Idea File

**August 1963** (partial)

The Greek Orthodox Church, I'm told, has a place in its Easter liturgy where everyone laughs. It's called, simply, the Rite of Laughter.*

\* \* \*

Good verse for the summer Bible conference circuit: "He hath filled the hungry with good things; and the rich He hath sent empty away" (Luke 1:53).

---

*\*Editor's note:* This was the inspiration for Dad's poem in *Psalms of My Life* titled, "A Psalm for Easter," which ends, "Laugh as if all the people in the whole world were invited to a picnic—and then invite them."

# Strange Birds in the Religion Department
## October 1963

One department of the modern American college, unlike the rest, doesn't often attempt to build on prior knowledge. That is religion, especially Protestant-oriented religion.

The physics professor—or even instructor—isn't likely to announce in his first lecture, "We must overcome your unfortunate and misleading introduction to this subject in high school." The math professor doesn't bewail prior indoctrination. History courses don't begin with sweeping negations or belittlement of previous study.

But religion is different. The usual religion professor, or dean of religion, says (or implies), "I shall not be satisfied until you tear down your past religious beliefs and begin to build afresh."

Such a professor takes each new student as a personal challenge, a contestant in the arena of dogma. And the more conservative the student's background, the greater is the professor's attempt to proselytize.

Another is the wide-eyed marveler: (female) "Goodness, child, I thought such ideas were confined to Tennessee. Surely you didn't grow up in California, did you?" (male) "You seem intelligent, son. You didn't say your home church was—er—Presbyterian, did you?"

Several species of *Avis religio campus* may be observed this fall. One is the blue-tailed bittern: "I once believed as you do—my father was a fundamentalist preacher. You know, no-fun-all-damn-and-no-mental. But that was before my intellectual enlightenment. And I think you too will find college a fascinating experience . . . if you keep an open mind."

Then there's the spoon-billed humbler: "Have you given up the search for truth? Do you really think you know enough to be able to say, 'I have arrived. I no longer am searching for truth.' Where, my boy, is your humility? Who can ever say he has found that for which humanity has searched for millennia?"

The red-headed shocker is rare, but not extinct: "I don't care what they taught you in Sunday school or youth meetings back home. What in heaven did you come to college for if you thought you already knew it all? Listen, are you taking zoology? Genetics? Try telling Schleider you believe in a virgin birth.—Now let's begin to construct a mature system of values."

Too often these men are successful in undermining prior convictions. It's a wise student who sees that their negations are as dogmatic as the system they attack, and their theological construction as dependent upon presuppositions—but without the authority of Jesus Christ and God's Word and the Christian Church to support them.

\* \* \*

A few years ago, Bryan Green (Church of England preacher) was invited to speak at an outstanding women's college in the Eastern United States. While he acknowledged his respect for other religions in his sermon, Canon Green nonetheless gave a clear explanation of Christianity's doctrinal content. He used a definition of Christianity suggested by Dr. Herbert Farmer: "Belief in Jesus Christ as absolute demand and final succor."

The results could have come out of the book of Acts. The college chaplain criticized Mr. Green for attacking other people's religion—because he dared to define Christianity. According to the chaplain, this showed Mr. Green's own basic insecurity pattern, even as Jesus' attack on the Pharisees showed His insecurity, leading Him to the rashness of the Cross, "which He would have avoided if He had affirmed life."

A student wrote in the campus newspaper that Canon Green's "even being allowed to speak on campus did violence to the student's freedom of religion."

The instructor in religion said that Mr. Green (formerly a chaplain at Oxford University) was like a "Holy roller from the South, with an intellectual slant." Then she told her classes that "a Mohammedan or a Buddhist could be as good a Christian as Mr. Green."

That was one time the birds screeched and the feathers flew. Would to God it would happen more often.

# *Passover Eve*
## April 1964

*What waste!*

> *This ointment, precious, here outpoured,*
> *Is treasure great beyond our minds to think.*
> *For years, until this moment, it was safe,*
> *Contained, awaiting careful use.*
> *Now broken, wasted, lost.*
*The world is poor.*

> *So poor it needs each drop of such a store.*
> *This treasure sold might feed a multitude*
> *For all their days.*
> *—This world is poor? It's poorer now*
> *The treasure's lost. Breathe deep*
> *Its fragrance; soon even that will cease,*
> *Except perhaps on hands that poured it out.*
*What purpose served?*

> *The act is void of reason, sense,*
> *Madmen do such deeds, not sane.*
> *Sane men hoard their treasure, spend with care:*
> *If good, to feed the poor; or else*
> *To feed themselves.*

> *Let her alone.*
> *She gives to me what you would give the world.*
> *You cannot understand such waste,*
> *She wonders that at such a time you'd choose*
> *The poor. Her guilt not waste, but love.*
> *She knows the value, you the cost,*
> *Of treasure she possessed, not you;*
> *And poured out on my head, my feet,*
> *Against tomorrow, when I die, and next day*
> *Fragrance fresh, renewed.**

# *Join the Church and Escape*
## June 1964

In his letter to the *New Yorker,* James Baldwin said that everybody has to have "an out"—dope, sex, alcohol. "Mine was the church."

Several years ago, the Protestant chaplain at an Eastern university was letting off steam. "Know the evangelical answer to a world crisis? Fill a ship with Christians, take a cruise to the Caribbean, and spend each morning listening to a Bible teacher give prophetic messages."

One major denomination held a convention in Birmingham recently. A professor at the denomination's main seminary said, "I couldn't go, but I looked forward with keen anticipation to the report that was issued afterward. When it came, I read that there was unusual unity at the convention—greater than they had experienced in recent years. And why was there such remarkable

---

*Editor's note:* This poem was the result of Dad's mourning the death of his third and oldest son, Joseph Tate Bayly V, who died on January 19, 1964. A slightly revised version of the poem is published in Dad's *Psalms of My Life* under the title, "A Psalm on the Death of an Eighteen Year Old Son."

unity? The report answered that one, too: 'We found no issues.' They met in Birmingham, and they found no issues!"*

Religion, according to Lenin, is the opiate of the people. We deny the description, and fulfill it. The church is our "out," our shelter, our escape from the battle that is against us.

But wasn't the Church intended to be a shelter? A bivouac, yes; occasionally a rest center behind the lines. But not nirvana, tranquilizing isolation. The Church is a tent pitched on the battlefield, not a vacation spot. The Church is a warship sailing mined waters, not a cruise ship following the Gulf Stream.

Every so often a shell rips through the tent. And the warship sometimes hits a mine. Dangerous? Yes, but who ever said the Church was safe? Certainly not its Lord. He seemed to indicate that Hell itself would break upon His Church, but would not prevail (Matt. 16:18).

This description of the Church would sound strange to most of our contemporaries. The Church, especially the evangelical sector, is hardly known for its involvement in battle. On some mission fields, perhaps, but not in the United States and Canada. Here we are holding meetings and counting attendance and carrying on scholastic disputations over whether Tribulation will some day strike the Church or not.

How many Christians attend the church meetings because they'd be lost without an unending Christian something-to-do? How many take their vacations at a Christian camp or on a Christians-only cruise because they'd be unable to cope with neutral atmosphere?

I think that we expect more from the Church than we should at times of personal tragedy. The function of the Church is not merely to console, to provide a shelter; it is to say, "Now get back out there and fight. You don't need to know the why of it all. All you need to know is that there's a war on." The Church should hold people not by serving as an opiate in times of sorrow, but by

---

*Birmingham, Alabama, was the center of the civil-rights conflict waged during these years. Eight months before the publication of this article, in September of 1963, Birmingham's Sixteenth Street Baptist Church was bombed during Sunday school classes, killing four African-American children.

getting them out of the hospital and back into battle as soon as possible.

Comfort that comes only from being around the Church, strength that depends on the rest center, is fragile at best. (Some of the grandest passages in missionary literature are Adoniram Judson turning from Ann Haseltine Judson's coffin to his discouraging work, and Hudson Taylor returning to the lonely battle after Maria died.)

In many ways, foreign missions have been our salvation during the past twenty years. It has been the missionary program of the typical evangelical church that has kept it from total isolation. Missionaries have forced us to learn geography and world affairs. (What would the Church care about the Congo or Vietnam apart from missionaries' being there?) Missionaries have stirred our conscience over abounding materialism and self-centeredness.

Last week a church editor told several of us, "I had a colostomy a few years ago—the growth was malignant. Later I met an old war-horse who told me, 'Good. Thank God for it. You don't begin to live until you know you're going to die.'"

Dying men aren't afraid of their reputations. And they throw everything into the battle. "So teach us to number our days, that we may apply our hearts unto wisdom" (Ps. 90:12).

# Small World, Isn't It?

## July 1964

The country has been stirred in recent weeks by one of those journalistic coincidences: a series of news stories with a disturbingly similar pattern.

First it was a young woman stabbed to death over a thirty-minute period, before thirty-eight spectators, in a quiet Queens,

N.Y., neighborhood. Next it was another girl, naked and helpless, who fought off her daylight attacker in a Bronx, N.Y., doorway— this time before forty spectators, deaf to her pleas for help. Then it was a crowd that watched silently as two nine-year-old boys drowned, not heeding the desperate cries for help of a man who was trying to save them.

Experts in the study of human behavior have their explanations. One is the major change during this century in America from a farming-community to an industrial-city culture. Man's concern for his neighbor has been severely strained by the change, with consequent depersonalization of relationships. "Let the authorities take care of problems—that's what they're paid for" approximates the change in attitude.

Another explanation is fear of involvement: "Why should I stick my neck out?"

Still another factor mentioned is the fear of injury or loss. Modern man wants to play it safe, avoid risks to life and limb. "Look, I might get hurt if I tried to do anything."

\* \* \*

The Army investigation of Korean war prisoners ten years ago provided some advance notice of this changed American outlook.

Take the court-martial of James C. Gallagher, granted the most notorious case. Here are the allegations, on the basis of which Gallagher was sentenced to life imprisonment.

*Specification 1:* In that Sergeant (then Corporal) James C. Gallagher, US Army . . . did, at Prisoner of War Camp No. 5, in the vicinity of Pyoktong, North Korea, on or about February 1951 murder Corporal Donald Thomas Baxter, an American prisoner of war, by means of forcibly ejecting him from his place of shelter and causing him to be exposed to extremely cold temperature, the said Corporal Donald Thomas Baxter at that time being sick, infirm with dysentery, and unable to help himself.

*Specification 2:* A similar crime, this time against Corporal John William Jones.

*Specification 3:* Gallagher did, on or about March, 1951, murder an American prisoner of war, name unknown, by means of striking him about the body; by forcibly ejecting him from his place of shelter—the final act of murder being similar to the previous two.

An Army psychiatrist, Colonel Meyer, commented on his findings in connection with this case somewhat as follows:

"Gallagher didn't bother us. There will always be Gallaghers.

"What did bother us were the other men, the fellows who shared the same prison hut with Gallagher and the men he murdered. After they returned to the States, they all told us the same stories about Gallagher—what he had done.

"These men were there the nights Gallagher threw the sick fellows outside. 'Did you see him do it?' we asked. 'Yes, sir,' they answered. 'Did you know it was so cold a man would die in a short time from exposure if he was thrown out of the hut?' 'Yes, we knew that.'

"'Soldier,' we asked, 'did you try to stop Gallagher? Did you do anything, say anything to try to keep him from murdering those men?' 'No, sir, I didn't.' 'Why didn't you, Soldier?' 'I felt it was none of my business . . . I didn't want to get involved . . . It was an awfully cold night.'"

Colonel Meyer considered this attitude evidence of an alarming breakdown in the home-training and education of these men, most of them young.

\*    \*    \*

But these explanations (the change in American culture, fear of involvement, fear of injury) don't explain the spectator angle, the silent watch behind darkened windows as an attacker returns twice to complete his mission of death by stabbing; the quiet onlookers as two boys drown.

I believe Americans have become inured to acts of violence by constant exposure to such acts in entertainment.

We have become voyeurs of violence.

People who enjoy three or four pretend killings a night in

their living room will scarcely react with revulsion on a Sunday morning as Jack Ruby really kills a manacled prisoner in that same living room.*   And if there's a good half-hour stabbing outside their living room at 3:00 A.M. on Monday morning, surely those same people will enjoy such a late-late show.

And who wants to interrupt a good show to make a phone call . . . even to the police . . . especially if the call will end the violence.

To me, the horrifying perversion of these years is that children of all ages, and teenagers, are exposed to the same acts of violence in the living room. And Christian homes are no exception.

"Whatsoever things are pure, whatsoever things are lovely, whatsoever things are of good report; if there be any virtue, and if there be any praise, think on these things" (Phil. 4:8). This is a command of God; we disobey it at the risk of disaster.

*       *       *

"The world has shrunk today." It is often said with reference to jet travel and fast communication.

—shrunk to the size of a twenty-three-inch screen.

—shrunk to the superficial, the mediocre, the relative.

—shrunk to a body without a soul, sex without a home, death without having lived.

—shrunk to joyless pleasure.

—shrunk to uglified beauty, beautified ugliness.

—shrunk to the twilight of meaning, the night of morals, a bright day of violence.

—shrunk to two dimensions, one generation, one time.

—shrunk to a little me.

It's a small world.

---

*Editor's note:* The Bayly household never had television.

# Great Doors Swing on Small Hinges

**May 1965**

One afternoon in the fall of 1949, a distinguished visitor from England came to my office in the Germantown section of Philadelphia. He was Dr. Arthur Taylor, retired master at the Chefoo Boys' School of the China Inland Mission.

Dr. Taylor was a fascinating conversationalist, and I thoroughly enjoyed his visit. He told of wartime duties for the British government, when—as a Church of Scotland cleric—he officially welcomed crews of Royal Navy ships on their return to England. And he reminisced of earlier days in China.

We were interrupted by a phone call for Dr. Taylor. The C.I.M. office (also in Germantown) had transferred the call to my office.

I heard his warm greeting, "Hello, Henry," before I left the office while he talked.

After the call was completed and I had returned, Dr. Taylor explained, "That was Henry Luce, one of my boys at Chefoo. On my way through New York I stopped at his office to see him, but he was out of town. He has just returned and called to welcome me to the States, and express his regret at missing my visit."

I have not forgotten this incident for a reason that I shall mention later, but it was also recently recalled to me by an article on the founder and publisher of the *Time-Life* complex of magazines in the *Saturday Evening Post*. There Luce was quoted about the Chefoo School: "I hated it and I loved it. The school was very religious and very rough and tough. After Chefoo, I found the getting of A's at Yale was for me a relatively easy matter."

(Incidentally, another famous alumnus of little Chefoo is contemporary author Thornton Wilder.)

At the time of Dr. Taylor's visit that fall afternoon in 1949, some evangelistic meetings were being held in a tent a continent away. Those meetings in Los Angeles catapulted a little-known evangelist, Billy Graham, to national and international prominence.

Why?

The commonly accepted explanation is William Randolph Hearst's terse telegram, to the editors of his newspapers across the country: "Puff Graham." And doubtless this was a crucial action, for Billy Graham immediately began to receive national coverage in the Hearst papers.

But this has not seemed a sufficient or complete explanation to some professional journalists who remember that in those days there was a deep well of resentment against Hearst in the American press—his name had become synonymous with a certain type of journalism. So the order, "Puff Graham," could easily have been the kiss of death to the young evangelist.

However, a few weeks after Dr. Taylor's visit *Life* magazine published a wholly favorable photo-spread on Billy Graham's Los Angeles campaign. It seemed to me at the time, and I still think, that *Life*—rather than Hearst—turned the tide of public attention in the evangelist's direction.

Why did *Life* react favorably to Billy Graham, and why has *Time-Life* generally had a more open and friendly attitude toward evangelical doctrine and causes in the past fifteen years than earlier?

I don't know for sure . . . but I wonder if God didn't use Dr. Taylor's American visit to stir the coals of Henry Luce's memory of a little school in China. For Chefoo wasn't all tough work. It was also masters who prayed for boys and tried to win them to Jesus Christ.

Some great doors swing on small hinges, so small that they can hardly be discerned at the time. The Sovereign God sets the hinges in their place: this, and not our ability to perceive God's will, is our confidence for guidance.

# The Truth—
# But Not the Whole Truth
## November 1965

The question of authority is basic to any religious system. And so we ask what authority is claimed and recognized by the contemporary evangelical Christian movement in the United States and Canada.

This seems to be one question that can be rather easily answered. Our authority is the Bible, the written Word of God. Anything more than this lacks authority, anything less than the whole Bible is insufficient.

A good, sound, biblical answer. But unfortunately the answer does not accurately describe the existing situation.

Part of the trouble goes back to the time sixty years ago when *The Fundamentals* were first published. Despite our affection for the first fundamentalists and our respect for what they did, we must admit that fundamentalism was never a biblical word, and perhaps was overloaded from the very beginning.

It is at least possible that, with the best of intentions, those Christians who developed and defended the concept of certain "fundamentals" were adopting an extra-biblical (or even a non-biblical) defense for the biblical position. For when they decided that certain teachings of the Bible were "fundamental," other doctrines were automatically relegated to a position that was less than fundamental (or basic). And so, as a result of their value judgment, the fundamentals tended to become definitive of the Christian position . . . even a half-century later.

In other words, from the very beginning of the movement, the danger was present that a human construct ("the fundamentals") would be accepted in place of the complete Bible from which that construct arose.

These fundamentals are and always have been basic to biblical Christianity. But when they became more or less codified as the "fundamental" doctrines of Christian belief, the assumption was almost unconsciously present that other teachings of the Bible are of secondary importance, and therefore may be neglected or even passed over.

Perhaps the deteriorating doctrine of the Church during these decades is to be ascribed, partially at least, to the fact that this particular doctrine was not included among the fundamentals. And then there's Christian love: if we listen to Jesus Christ in the Gospels, we cannot escape the conclusion that love of the brethren here and now is as fundamental to Christian life as belief in the Second Coming. But Christian love was omitted from the fundamentals, while the Second Coming was included. Is there any relationship between this omission and the generally accepted image of American evangelical Christianity as a bitter, self-centered, fighting movement? We are known for our belief in the Second Coming, but not for our love.

Of course, *The Fundamentals* represented only one factor in this twentieth-century doctrinal crystallization, although it was the most far-reaching. (Several million of the volumes were distributed free of charge to 300,000 ministers, missionaries, and other workers throughout America and around the world.) Another significant factor was the increasing use of various "Bases of Faith" as a test of orthodoxy and common ground for interdenominational activity.

Historically, these bases (or doctrinal standards) had their origin at the Niagara Bible Conference early this century, and the Niagara Platform has served as the pattern for numerous other Christian movements that have not been denominationally related. By narrowing the field of Christian doctrines down to a workable five or ten, these Bible conferences, foreign missionary societies, and other agencies and institutions have found a test of orthodoxy that is relatively easy to apply and implement. But in the process, disproportionate weight has come to be attached to doctrines explicitly stated in the doctrinal basis, as over against other doctrines not explicitly stated therein.

Some answer this by pointing out that these bases of faith usually begin with an affirmation of belief in biblical inspiration; therefore all other biblical doctrines are implicitly included. This is so, but if the first statement is sufficient to cover all biblical doctrines, why are specific ones singled out for inclusion thereafter?

And so we have come to accept an eclectic type of authority in evangelical Christianity. We select certain doctrines as constitutive and others as secondary. As a concomitant, those books of the Bible that emphasize the fundamental doctrines are given preferred positions in our canon of teaching emphasis and preaching.

Why have the Synoptic Gospels, with their record of the life of Christ, been neglected by many Christian churches, while such books as Romans and Revelation are given prominence? Why is John's Gospel so much more familiar than his Epistles? Why is the Epistle of James less popular than the Epistle to the Hebrews?

In the thinking of believers, what is the effect of sixty years of singling out the deity of Christ as fundamental, while bypassing His humanity and the unity of His nature?

Most of us are seriously concerned about the lowering levels of ethics and morality among evangelical Christians. Is the absence of the doctrine of Law from *The Fundamentals* and doctrinal bases relevant?

I do not intend to make whipping boys out of the writers of *The Fundamentals*—Gray, Orr, Thomas, Torrey, et al.—whose shoes I am not worthy to tie. The fault lies with us, who accepted their masterful answer to heresy in their day as the code of our belief.

The Bible does not lend itself to abridgment or underlining, except at the expense of authority.

# *When Man Tries to Copy God*

## December 1965

Once upon this earth, a race of men set out to copy God.

Place-bound, they sought the secret of His omnipresence. Laying rails, they sped from here to there; a continent that took their fathers months to cross was theirs in days.

Their sons forsook the rails, and land itself, and cut the days to hours. And the bold among their children went out beyond the necessary air and, encapsulated, compassed the continent—and circled earth itself—in minutes.

*Man, you threaten not my omnipresence.*

Wisely, this race of men perceived that physical limits denied them the secret of divine omnipresence. A body must be here or there, not both. Not even an important body can be in all theres in one now.

And so they laid cables beneath the separating seas, flashed coded words with speed of light. Their sons sent words themselves through air, and voices spoke of love and money, news, threats, and organization.

The sons' children winged pictures with the sound, so that the now of Rome became the now of Denver—Pope and premier, jester and President were in all the homes, talking, smiling, frowning, talking. But not listening nor feeling.

Nor seeing. The greatest minds could only cope with limited impressions, gray bowls of custard too small to hold a universe of facts.

*Man, you threaten not my omniscience.*

So men built great machines to count, to recall, to act: slow thought replaced by super-fast electronics. They made fibers that covered legs like skin. They made a bomb and scuba suits and sewed an arm back on. They made mountains of wheat and a pill.

They brought the Philadelphia Orchestra and the Beatles and Joan Baez into sixty million living rooms, for command performances.

They dropped their armies from the sky. They sailed their ships beneath the waves. Their soldiers flew and fought and died.

Died?

Their thinkers thought and planned and died.

Their big ones died, in youth or age.

*Man, you threaten not my omnipotence.*

After several generations, frustrated in their attempt to copy God, this race of men seriously began to question His reality.

Where is He? The name stands for the unknown. Perhaps there are only he's.

Maybe there is no God who is omniscient, -present, -potent. Could he be only a target to help improve our aim?

Death we know. Kennedy, Churchill, National Safety Council, cancer, fallout, coronaries. Death is real.

Despair is real.

Computers are real.

But God real?

Honesty compels us to deny God.

\*　　\*　　\*

One man there was, a craftsman who never touched a power saw, even. Never traveled beyond the little state in which he was born. Owned no shares of stock, or real estate, or an automobile.

He said, You've got it all wrong.

If you're going to copy God, copy Him—copy *Him,* not copy His attributes.

What's He like? Not a computer or a two-way TV or a supersonic jet. He's not omnipotence, omniscience, omnipresence.

God is love.

When you love, you're like Him—not when you build a computer.

You can lunch in New York and have dinner in San Francisco and take an overdose of sleeping pills at the Mark Hopkins.

Perfect love gets despair off your back—not a jet flight or the power money buys.

Despair is real. Death is real. But so is God. And there's only one thing more important than God is love. That is, God loves you. Loves you as you ought to love your children, your wife. To God, you are of more value than many computers.

Do you want to love God? Well, you start by admitting that you're only a creature. . . .

# The Teaching We Have Neglected

**January 1966**

Twelve or fifteen years ago, the late Canon T. C. Hammond of the Church of England visited the United States. Toward the end of his trip, in which he visited many parts of the country, I asked Canon Hammond for his predominant impression of evangelical Christianity in America. The author of Inter-Varsity Fellowship's *Reasoning Faith* and *In Understanding Be Men,* and authority on Roman Catholic theology (*The Hundred Texts,* published by Irish Church Missions) seemed unusually qualified to render an objective judgment on such a matter.

His answer was prompt: He was impressed by our shallow treatment of the doctrines of sin and law. We seemed to introduce children and adults to grace and salvation without laying any adequate foundation in the knowledge of personal rebellion and sin.

The result, he said, was a low view of Christ and grace and righteousness, for our appreciation of salvation is in direct relation to our understanding of the pit of sin from which we were dug.

In answer to a further question, Canon Hammond agreed that a low level of personal righteousness and sensitivity to sin among American Christians might be related to the same cause. Wasn't that what the Apostle Paul was talking about when he said, "I had not known sin, but by the law: for I had not known lust, except the law had said, Thou shalt not covet" (Rom. 7:7).

\* \* \*

Who's responsible for the present erosion of American morality and personal ethics? It's easy to blame the days in which we live . . . Hugh Hefner and his *Playboy* philosophy . . . the end times.

When the shoe is on the other foot, whether in England after the Wesleys, or America after the Great Awakening, we know the answer: revival in the Church brought about a quickening of the world's standards of morality. The salt had its effect on society.

And today? The Church that takes credit for heightened social morality must acknowledge its responsibility for society's moral depression. Perhaps the salt has lost its savor (Matt. 5:13, 14).

This brings us back to Canon Hammond's thesis. If the children of the Church have not been taught God's standards of righteous living, the children of the world have nothing against which to measure their conduct.

\* \* \*

But why has this teaching been neglected? Why have children grown up in the Church and in Christian homes without a solid foundation in the biblical doctrines of law and sin?

At the risk of being misunderstood, may I suggest that it has been because of our obsession during the past thirty or forty years with the immediacy of salvation. We have had one continual message for our children: "Ye must be born again" (John 3:7). Every Sunday school lesson has been turned into a salvation lesson; decisions have been the response constantly sought.

We have not taught the Bible with integrity: John's Gospel as John's Gospel; Proverbs as Proverbs; Judges as Judges; Exodus 20 as Exodus 20. Instead we have taught John's Gospel as John's Gospel; Proverbs as John's Gospel; Judges as John's Gospel; Exodus 20 as John's Gospel . . . if we have taught the latter at all.

Recently I had a letter from a woman who related her experience teaching Ruth to junior highs the Sunday before. "Suddenly it came to me that what my girls needed wasn't that they should love Christ as Ruth loved Naomi, but that they should be the sort of women when they grow up that Naomi was to stir such a response of love in her daughter-in-law. Ruth was profitable as Scripture itself, not just as a type of Christ—valid though that might be."

What our children (and we ourselves) need is exposure to the whole Bible in its integrity, "for doctrine, for reproof, for correction, for instruction in righteousness: That the man of God may be perfect, thoroughly furnished unto all good works" (2 Tim. 3:16, 17).

In the Westminster Shorter Catechism, the Presbyterian Church taught children those doctrines it considered necessary to glorify and enjoy God. The doctrines were arranged according to the pattern of biblical revelation. Thus the sweep and scope of God's revelation in history became the sweep and scope of God's revelation to the child.

A few years ago, Dr. J. C. Macaulay, president of London (Ontario) Bible College, told of an incident when he visited the Scottish islands of the Hebrides, where revival had been endemic for some time. Dr. Macaulay was on his way to a church service and heard a low wailing noise from a cottage.

In response to the visitor's question, a man with whom he was walking replied, "That's William, finding his way to God. He'll come through."

If we trust God's Spirit to bring our children through to

salvation . . . in His time . . . we will with patience teach law and depravity and sin and providence and all the other doctrines of Scripture, as the foundation of salvation that means something in moral living, and of an exalted view of Christ.

If, on the other hand, we seek above all else the security of knowing that our children have made a decision, on the basis of which we can reassure them of their salvation from a very early age, we shall probably continue to have spiritual mediocrity and a-nomianism (if not antinomianism) in the Church.

I believe that some children will be saved early in life. But others—even in the same family—will come later. In God's providence, all fruit does not ripen at the same time.

# Oh, for an Honest Hymnbook

## July 1966 (partial)

*If our hymns were based on our actual practice rather than our aspirations, maybe we'd have such new hymns as "Goof the good goof," or "Sit down, O men of God."*

Maybe we need an honest hymnbook.

I remember, years ago, a children's day service when the minister's two boys—age four and six—sang a duet:

> *Years I spent in vanity and pride*
> *Caring not my Lord was crucified.*

But that's not the problem with our hymns. Those boys didn't set out to sing something they didn't mean; some adult made the unfortunate choice for them.

An honest hymnbook would revise the old familiar words to say what people really mean. For instance:

*Take my life and let it be*
*Yes let it be, Lord, let it be.*

*When morning gilds the skies*
*My heart awaking cries*
*O no, another day.*

*O for a thousand tongues to sing*
*My great Redeemer's praise*
*One tongue is hardly any use*
*So I'll my voice not raise.*

*Amazing grace, how sweet the sound*
*That saved a wretch like you.*

*Speak, Lord, in the babble*
*While I'm occupied.*

*Am I a soldier of the Cross?*
*No, I my card have burned.*

*In Christ there is no East or East,*
*in Him no South or South."*

*Sit down, O men of God*
*Have done with greater things.*

*Shall I empty-handed be*
*When retirement I shall see.*

*My hope is built on nothing less*
*Than God is dead and the new morality.*

*I love to tell the story*
*Of things I see below.*

*Goof the good goof*
*With all thy might.*

# Oh, for the Good Old Days

... when one knew that America was far superior to Russia, where marriage was only a physical bond, the Bible was banned from the schools, and the people's lives were government-controlled from birth to death

**August 1966**

When I was growing up, I remember, we were impressed by our elders with the evil results of Communist doctrine in Russia.

Marriage was one example. Under Communism, the home was breaking up. Divorce had become a simple civil matter, available to any couple who no longer wished to live together.

Free love was widespread in Russia, we were told. Unmarried men and women could openly have relations without stigma. Moral standards that had formerly controlled attitudes and actions were no longer considered relevant, now that Communism was the dominant ideology.

The training of children was considered the responsibility of the state. Nursery schools had been established for Russian children three or four years old, and their mothers were no longer burdened with responsibility for them. The state also assumed the care of children born out of marriage, the result of casual liaisons.

Freedom from responsibility for their children meant that women could take full-time positions alongside their husbands. I remember news pictures of women repairing streets, then later, of women in scientific laboratories. The new Communist law forbade any job discrimination based on sex.

I recall a series of posters, given me by an elder in the church—perhaps he was my Sunday school teacher—depicting the Communist attitude toward God. One had a crudely drawn coffin in which lay an old, dirty, white-haired man. The Russian characters on the front of the Photostat were translated into English on the reverse side: "God died when Communism freed the people. Nobody needs God any more. God, rest in your coffin."

We were also told that Communism had destroyed personal initiative in Russia. The government was reaching into all areas of life, from the cradle to the grave, and controlling whatever it touched.

And God had been banished from Russian life. I remember a Jewish teacher, a man, in West Philadelphia High School, who would read the prescribed number of Bible verses for the day in homeroom period—always from the Psalms—with deep respect. As he closed the Bible, he often said, "Under Communism, this would be impossible. There they have banned the Holy Books."

All this was evidence, according to our elders, of the demonic nature of Communism. If America ever became Communistic, we were told, these same results would follow. Thank God America was still Christian and still a democracy.

\*     \*     \*

These memories were evoked by an item in the newspaper the other day. An important official in the federal government's Health, Education and Welfare department said that the education of four-year-olds would soon be compulsory. We know today, he said, that character (this is the word he used) is formed very early, and so children should be in school at least by the age of four. Otherwise we miss out on the most crucial period of a child's life for training.

Reading the official's words, and a subsequent confirmatory statement by President Lyndon B. Johnson, I considered the United States today, a generation later. Our government has not become Communistic, yet we have entered into a period of social, economic, educational, and moral conditions similar to those we were told were the result of Communism in Russia.

One important difference is that the Church in the United States has not been suppressed, as in Russia and China, so that the new order might be established. Instead, the Church, through many of its leaders, has gone along with the changes, even providing a theological rationale for some of them.

Well, at least we still have more telephones and color television sets than Communist Russia. And more Bibles.

# Is There a Parallel Between Infant Baptism and Early Decisions for Jesus?

**December 1966** *(partial)*

Have you ever considered the possibility of a parallel between infant baptism or confirmation, on the one hand, and early "decisions for Christ" on the other?

Most of us evangelicals fear an act of religious formality early in life that may be trusted in the absence of conversion. "Of course I'm a Christian—I was confirmed at the age of twelve" rings an alarm in our minds.

But "Of course I'm a Christian—I raised my hand in a children's meeting" doesn't set off the same alarm.

Some parents and teachers go even further, trying to convince the doubting teenager that he's really a Christian, because "you asked Jesus to come into your heart in the primary department." Assurance comes from the adult who remembers an act, rather than from the Spirit who may—or may not—indwell the life.

Not all doubts are bad. Doubt may be God's instrument of conviction, and to turn it off by reminding the doubter of a prior act—whether confirmation or hand-raising—may be to perform eternal disservice to his soul.

Even in Christian homes, there are individual differences. Not all children will necessarily trust Christ in childhood. Historically, Polycarp (martyred when he was over eighty) and Jonathan Edwards (spearhead of colonial America's Great Awakening) knew Christ before the age of ten. But Augustine, son of godly Monica, and John Wesley, child of the parsonage and of strong Christian parents, both were around thirty years of age when they converted. For Adoniram Judson, the occasion was a summer between college and seminary.

Somehow most of us feel that if the crop isn't harvested at least by the teen age, there's not much hope. And many Christian parents would settle for the comforting assurance that their child "made his decision when he was thirteen," even if a life of spiritual mediocrity followed, rather than go through the hurt and blind faith in God until their child comes Home from the far country with true spiritual power.

# The Missing Ingredient in the New Bibles

**February 1967**

This year the Revised Standard Version of the Bible comes of age. And in these twenty-one years since its publication, a plethora of other translations and paraphrases has been produced.

Each represents a particular viewpoint and satisfies a part of the market.

None satisfies every group. The monopoly of King James

and Douay in Protestantism and Roman Catholicism has ended during this generation.

In their place we now have, in addition to the RSV (which, in America at least, is the dominant new version), a considerable list of options: *The New English Bible New Testament;* Kenneth Taylor's paraphrases; *Today's English Version* of the New Testament; *The New American Standard Version* (New Testament only thus far); Berkeley; Williams; Beck; the Knox and Confraternity (Roman Catholic); and some fragments, such as *God is for Real, Man* (inner city).

Just published is *The Jerusalem Bible* (Roman Catholic). In the planning stages are two evangelical committee efforts: *The New American Standard Old Testament*; and a second, yet to be named.

I suppose that I should rejoice at this proliferation, and I do. "Everyman" in America, 1967, should be able to read God's Word in the idiom he understands, rather than in that of his ancestors almost 400 years ago.

But proliferation may lead to confusion. And choice may lead to privatism. And a glut of Bread in America may dull our sensitivity to the hundreds of millions elsewhere who lack even a crumb.

I can't help thinking of what the same amount of time, money, and scholarly resources would have accomplished if they had been expended on missionary translation and Bible distribution.

Why should I own ten different Bibles when my brother doesn't even have a verse?

But bypassing that uncomforting aspect, here are some of the problems that I see in the present embarrassment of biblical riches. You may want to add to the list, or suggest compensating values that I may be assuming.

(1) Confusion has resulted. The Bible's use in public worship has been complicated by the variety of versions and paraphrases in the congregation. Bible memorization has become a knotty problem, especially with children.

(2) A subjective element is present in all translations, but especially in one-man translations and paraphrases. The evangeli-

cal Christian public is quite aware of this problem when it comes to the RSV: "young woman" in Isaiah 7:14, which was the *cause célèbre* for rejecting this version, even burning it, in the late 1940s.

But while the front door was being zealously guarded against the RSV, the back door was left open to all comers. Evangelical attitudes toward every other Bible production have been almost a-critical, by contrast.

So we accept—in place of the inspired Scripture—a fictitious, allegorized hash of Song of Solomon in the *Amplified.* We seem to have no objections to changing the all-embracing term "salvation" to the limited "bring you to heaven" (Rom. 1:16) in *Living Letters.* And the latter in a day when Christian morals and ethics are declining, and God's present saving work in this evil world desperately needs emphasis.

Examples could be multiplied; I have merely chosen from two that are totally within the evangelical community. (Incidentally, some months ago I mentioned these two illustrations to the publishers.)

Every translation is an interpretation. A paraphrase, by nature, is even more interpretive. And the fact that God's Word is changed to correspond to evangelical thought patterns is hardly less blameworthy—perhaps more so, since we hold to the doctrine of inspiration—than that it is changed to reflect liberal bias.

(3) Committee translations, on the other hand, tend to be pedantic. W. H. Auden, the poet, found fault with the *New English Bible* on this score.

Who is least likely to be able to write in the current idiom, especially if you add the necessary dimensions of grace and beauty? I think there is little doubt, with few exceptions, that the answer is scholars. The man who translates from Hebrew and Greek, whether he is English or German or American, is not the man who has the gift to talk the language of Everyman.

Yet this is the necessary reason for any new translation. I doubt that many scholars would say that new manuscript discoveries, or changed linguistic concepts are of sufficient scope to necessitate another translation. It is rather the communication of God's Word in the 1967 American idiom.

Then why start with the scholars? Why not start with writers, who would use common sources—such as the King James and the American Standard of 1901, both of which are in the public domain—to render the Word of God in modern English. Then have the scholars check what the writers have produced against the original, returning the corrected manuscript to the writers for rewriting.

It seems to me that this is technically feasible, but that the other way around is not. Once scholars set the Word in concrete, capable writers would find it hard to breathe freshness—and to change the scholars' minds about the wording.

Before this new evangelical translation project gets too far down the track, I hope someone with influence (in the evangelical lowerarchy, this means money) says, "Look here, Committee on a New Translation of the Bible. Let's turn this thing over to some people like Frank Gaebelein and Elizabeth Elliot, maybe even W. H. Auden and John Updike, to see what they'd come up with. You'll have your innings on the rewrite. But give them a go at it first."*

Who knows, maybe the new Bible would come out beautiful as well as faithful to the original languages.

Recently we've been using *The Jerusalem Bible* (translated from the original languages, via the French) in family prayers. From youngest to oldest, we like it. Simplicity, beauty, clarity, power, felicity of expression are in the parts we've read.

J. R. R. Tolkien, British novelist and poet, is listed as one of the collaborators in its production.

---

*Editor's note:* The then unnamed translation is now known as the *New International Version (NIV)*, and as it turned out, Frank Gaebelein was one of the consultants for literary style.

# A Word to the Now Generation

**March 1967**

Dear "Twenty-five and Under,"

I see that *Time* has selected you "Man of the Year." Congratulations. You had it coming.

Maybe in twenty years, when you're the Older Generation, you'll make it again.

But I doubt it.

Then "Twelve and Under" will probably be their choice. The Pepsi Generation will yield to the Milk Generation in this race from age and experience to the ultimately influential ones— around 1990 or 2000—in the womb.

When you get to be forty or forty-five, the thirteen-to-twenty-fives will be the other generation. And you'll be senior citizens.

But this year, 1967, you're riding high on the hog, a hog we've tended and fattened for you.

Strangely, you've accepted the hog but rejected us.

Today I listened to one of your generation (not of my household) sound off on my generation. He did an outstanding diagnostic job. No, it was more than diagnosis: his knife laid the tissues bare. You have nothing to say to us, he said, you "speak with forked tongues," you say one thing and do another. We laugh at you, he went on, hoping some day you'll realize what you are. We have no respect for you, you've given us nothing to respect. But you won't even admit it. You should be honest, realize that you're hypocrites, and stop going around parading behind some self-righteous mask.

He didn't stop there. You older people see things black and white, he said, we see them in various shades of gray. You are Moral Absolutists (at least in your words), while we are Moral Relativists. You tell us to be good, and we say Shut up, what is good, who is good? To our generation the word stands for the unknown.

Sound familiar? The Under Twenty-five who spoke is a Christian, educated almost completely in Christian schools. So he wasn't talking about Mr. Secular or Mr. God is Dead. He was talking about Mr. Christian, about me.

My impulse is to defend my generation, to write about the Depression we experienced (instead of listening to Bob Dylan, Joan Baez, or some other millionaire—through your largess—sing about poverty), the wars, our struggle for an education, the sacrifices we watched our parents make—often, in the immediate, uncomprehending—to help us get an education or provide for needy relatives and neighbors. That was before the federal and local governments took over responsibility by our largess.

But I'll resist the impulse toward self-defense, just as my parents doubtless resisted similar impulses when I was growing up and giving them their lumps.

I'll agree with the Under Twenty-five who made these incisive comments today. We're hypocrites, my generation. We strain at gnats and swallow camels. We've fallen short of the absolutes we try to pass on to you.

We're a mess.

But what hurts the most is this: So are you. And I suspect that's why you're so bitter about us. You have to see the mess perpetuated in yourselves. You see your generation going down the same hypocritical path.

You can reject our hair styles. Our conformity, our ticky-tacky houses, crummy bourgeois tendencies, moral absolutes, music.

Deep down, don't you wish you could reject the hog as well, that 13 billion-dollar-a-year slice you personally spend? The soft living, plush houses, fast cars you like as much as we do?

Empty words.

Do as I sing, not as I do.

We're fakey, but so are you. You say everything's relative, you want us to look at you in shades of gray—but then you judge us by your own absolute standard of black and white.

Honesty is your prime virtue, if we hear you right. Then why all the cheating and shoplifting?

You don't mean honesty like that? You mean frankness, openness about sex and morals, no pretense?

You're just like us. Make up the rules as you go along. Boardwalk and Park Place are cheap, Baltic expensive. You don't like the penalty? Put it at the bottom of the pile and take another. Better yet, do away with the penalties.

Neither of us is happy, your generation or mine. No hypocrite ever is. The difference is that we're twenty years closer to the end of the game than you. And we're beginning to see that there's a Rulebook and a Judge who sees through us more clearly than even the Twenty-five and Unders.

And we are coming to see that a year passes quickly, that time is less important than eternity.

# *Support Your Local Prophet*
## March 1968

"**W**oe to you, scribes and Pharisees, hypocrites! for you build the tombs of the prophets and adorn the monuments of the righteous, saying, 'If we had lived in the days of our fathers, we would not have taken part with them in shedding the blood of the prophets'" (Matt. 23:29–30 RSV).

\* \* \*

Monument building is the religious equivalent of Monday morning quarter-backing and second-guessing the expert. We all indulge in it, all of us hypocrites.

We who would have been at the front of the prophet-killing mob join the tomb-adorning crowd. Then we turn away from the garlands we have hung, from our speeches of fulsome praise for the dead prophet, and proceed to kill a new one on our way home from the cemetery.

A law of religion seems to be, "Honor the dead prophet; kill the living one."

I suspect that our praise makes prophets tremble as much in death as spittle, prison, and rocks ever did in life.

Let's have a memorial service for a dead prophet. Join me in placing a wreath on Robert Raikes' tomb. The inscription on that particular gravestone reads, "English printer, proprietor of the *Gloucester Journal.* In 1780 Robert Raikes started the first Sunday school."

Hail to the founder of Sunday school! Today in the United States alone we have 294,618 Sunday schools, with 3,799,765 teachers and officers, and a total enrollment of 46,856,391. Hang a wreath on Robert Raikes' tomb!

But we are 188 years removed from that first Sunday school, derisively called "Raikes' Ragged School" by the Church people of his day.

In those days, Sunday school in England was attacked by no less a personage than the Archbishop of Canterbury. (From Jesus' time onward high priests and archbishops have had low prophet-recognition scores.)

America was no better, when the Sunday school movement crossed the Atlantic a decade later. One lady, who gathered some children to study the Bible in a church balcony in Connecticut, was rebuked by her minister with these words: "The Book is the enemy of learning."

The first Sunday schools were chased out of churches into storefronts, dance halls, factories, and homes. And Sunday school was historically a lay movement because the clergy refused to become involved.

The records of Boston's Park Street Church contain the following entry in 1817:

A number of Park Street Church members met in the vestry to discuss forming a Sunday School. Dr. Griffin, pastor, was present.

Objections: 1. It might be a desecration of the Sabbath. 2. Children ought to be instructed by their parents at home. 3. Professing Christians ought to be at home engaged in reading, meditation and prayer, instead of going abroad to teach the children of other families, on the Sabbath.

Answered: Sabbath-School teaching was a missionary work designed to gather from the streets and wharves, children who were neglected by their parents, and suffered to go abroad on the Sabbath, when generally engaged in play or mischief.

Conclusion: Decided to establish a Sunday school on Mason Street. First Superintendent was Mr. William Thurston [incidentally, the first name attached to the covenant of Park Street Church]."

The first Sunday school in the Park Street Church building itself was founded on December 13, 1819. Ten male and eleven female scholars were present that Sunday.

\*   \*   \*

I can't help wondering if the Park Street antagonists of Sunday school in 1817 might say, "See—we were right," if they could observe Sunday school in this century.

When Sunday school moved into the church, parents gradually abandoned their responsibility to instruct their own children at home. "Now the Church will do it—we don't need family prayers any longer, we don't need to teach our little ones."

And I wonder if the 1817 protagonists of Sunday school, if they could observe our present 9:45 A.M. Sunday school activities, would say, "We were wrong. Sunday school does not gather children from the streets and playgrounds; Sunday school is not for children who are neglected by their parents, children who are engaged in mischief."

If Robert Raikes were alive today, I think he'd probably be holding Friday Midnight School in Old Town, Haight-Ashbury, Yorkville, or the Village. Or maybe Saturday school in Harlem or South Chicago.

And he'd be just as much of a *persona non grata* to the religious community in 1968 as he was in 1780.

\* \* \*

We're surprised that a prophet was ever derided, libeled, imprisoned, excommunicated, killed for this idea or that, which we accept today. We marvel all the way home from the cemetery.

Let tombstone garlands rot. Support your local prophet.

Or admit, at least, that the idea you espouse may not be the same idea for which a man gave his reputation or his life.

# Are We Undermining Authority?

## May 1968

If there's been one doctrine strongly taught and defended by evangelicals during the past several decades, it's the inspiration of the Scriptures. Among many, perhaps most, who taught the doctrine, verbal inerrancy of the original manuscripts has been upheld.

Now with all this emphasis on inspiration and inerrancy, you'd think that young people who have grown up in an evangelical milieu would be firmly grounded in the Bible's authority.

They're not. In my experience, at least, I don't usually find the reflex, "The Bible says it and so it must be true," among young men and women.

The reaction of a student in a Christian college, on being

reminded that the Bible forbids premarital intercourse, is rather typical of the attitude I've found. "Maybe the Bible says it, but if it does, that isn't what it means."

The element of doubt about what the Bible teaches in areas of less emotional involvement is also significantly high among our evangelical teens and students. Does God have purpose in human suffering? Is God powerful enough to act today? Will Christ return to this earth? For a large number of evangelical young men and women, such questions are not settled by what the Bible says.

If my impressions are correct, we are in danger, period, since it is questionable whether morality and ethics—even faith (Rom. 10:17)—can stand, apart from the support of accepted biblical authority.

How do we explain this weak attitude toward the Bible's authority? Have we unwittingly undermined confidence in the Bible?

I think we have got things out of the right order, at least as far as ordinary Christians—especially the young—are concerned. We have stressed the Bible's inspiration and assumed that authority would take care of itself. But it hasn't.

Theologians may conclude that inspiration is the ground of authority, and therefore must come first. And they are probably right in a theological context.

J. Gresham Machen once said that theology begins with the doctrine of inspiration, while apologetics ends with it. I suspect, if this is so, that we have made the mistake of treating our young as theologians rather than as potential converts or young Christians.

I believe that the debate about biblical inerrancy during recent decades has had the unfortunate result of weakening the Bible's authority in the minds of the young. The possibility or impossibility of infinitesimal error has tended to obscure the great, overarching areas about which there is no question.

By arguing about whether there is dust on the piano, or whether the kitchen floor is completely clean, a husband will lower his children's overall impression of their mother's faithful loving service and diminish her authority in their eyes. When they are older, the children may see things in true perspective; then they

83

are likely to blame the picayune, judgmental father. But meanwhile the harm has been done.

So it may be with the authority of the Scriptures in the eyes of the young. We argue about whether 3,000 or 30,000 soldiers fought in a battle and we lose a greater battle.

Children, teens, and students need to be brought into Christ's kingdom by faith, by their own personally exercised choice. From a human standpoint, they need examples, adults who say and live the principle, "I believe the Bible." And I think this is the really important thing to communicate to the young—complete submission to the Bible's authority—rather than, "I believe in the inspiration of the Bible."

I know that full conviction of the Bible's authority over all of life comes through the Holy Spirit's work. But it is often, perhaps usually, communicated through the Christian community.

Perhaps this low view of Scripture's authority is related to a low view of Christ's authority. We may be reaping the results of recent decades when we appealed to the young to "receive Christ as Savior," bypassing His demand of absolute Lordship and doing violence to His Person.

A fresh breath of submission to the authority of Christ and the Scriptures in the Church, and in the lives of Christians—especially the young—could be the catalyst needed to change the world's drift toward anarchy and nihilism.

And I am not usually a prophet of doom.

# Does Christian Coffee Save Men?

**September 1968**

"Pre-evangelism" has become a familiar concept in these years.

We cannot assume that we have the respect or attention or interest of the person to whom we want to bring the life-giving Christ; we must earn these by entering his life, by becoming concerned about his whole person. The process by which we do this is pre-evangelism, breaking up the ground for seed we intend to plant.

This is a pendulum swing away from the former concept of "a tract, a testimony, a decision for or against." And in the opinion of most of us who were raised in an atmosphere of success stories about soul-winning conversations with total strangers on streetcars and trains, the swing is healthy.

We may not have formulated it, but the question at the back of our minds when we listened to those soul-winners was, "What about your children, your neighbors, your business and professional associates? Are you reaching them? Does the gospel stand exposure to more than a twenty-minute conversation on a streetcar, does it speak to 'life that is so daily?'"

We weren't hearing about conversions in the ongoing peer group of the soul-winners. It was the transient and casual situation that was presented as a pattern.

Street meetings, prison and rescue mission ministries were another part of the picture, a part that did not remove the question about Christianity's effectiveness with one's peers.

Now we have settled in to evangelize our neighbors and close associates and the first step is to gain a hearing.

So we pre-evangelize.

Great.

But when is the prefix removed? When does pre-evangelism turn into evangelism?

If it doesn't, the term is a misnomer. We may be displaying the fruits of righteousness, but we aren't evangelizing. We may be doing the good works God has commanded, but we are not evangelizing.

This is so in personal relationships and in group activities. A Christian coffee shop without evangelism is merely a coffee shop run by Christians, regardless of the high-sounding pre-evangelism theory that led to its establishment. Christian coffee doesn't save lost men.

Are we really concerned that men shall be saved? Are we convinced that they're lost? Are we certain that only Christ can save them?

When the pendulum was at the opposite extreme, the answer to those questions was in no doubt. It was the strong conviction that prompted train conversions and promoted street meetings.

Maybe the part of the spectrum covered by that former evangelism was limited, but it was covered. Maybe the presentation of the gospel was too either-or, too take-it-or-leave-it, but the effect was to communicate urgency.

Urgency. Strange, isn't it, that the word today is more applicable to the community of atomic scientists (who have just advanced their eschatological clock to seven minutes to twelve) than to the Christian community.

What is the goal of evangelism?

In the former day, it was simply stated: to save men from hell's eternal separation from God and take them to heaven.

On the way, things happened. But evangelism wasn't primarily to mend marriages or heal loneliness or solve life's problems. It was to get men right with God and settle an eternal destiny.

Do you sense that we have lost this dimension in much of our evangelism today, that our lingering at the way station of pre-evangelism is because we're not sure of the real destination?

It takes faith to believe that nice people are under God's judgment for sin, and that only Jesus Christ can save them. This faith is somehow different from faith that divorce can be avoided or problem drinking controlled. After all, marriage counselors and programs for alcoholics are achieving results without reference to any narrow Christian claims.

And we hate to be narrow in a day of widening highways.

Tolerance is the spirit of pre-evangelism. Evangelism says that there's only one road to God, and Jesus Christ is it; only one hope of heaven, the reconciling cross and empty tomb; only one saving response, believing what God has said in His Word about our sin and His Son. Even for nice peer-group people.

When everyone else is involved in an agonizing search, it's not easy to say, "I have found. Taste and see that the Lord is good." But that's evangelism.

# Compassion or Pity: Which Do You Show?

**March 1969**

Com-pas-sion [fr L *com-* with, + *pati* to bear, suffer]: sympathetic consciousness of others' distress together with a desire to alleviate it.

pity [fr L *pietat* piety]: sympathetic sorrow for one suffering, distressed or unhappy.

\* \* \*

A scale of human virtues today would probably rank compassion rather low. Pity would be high.

What's the difference, since both involve sympathy and sorrow for the distressed person?

It's in that little phrase, "together with a desire to alleviate the distress."

Few Americans would have the reaction of one man who saw pictures of emaciated, hollow-eyed starving children on TV and said, "They ruined my breakfast."

Almost everybody pities the children. And with no small pity.

But only a few feel compassion. In the words that were used of our Lord, they are "moved with compassion" (Mark 1:41)— moved to contribute to Biafran relief.

Pity is a dangerous emotion. It inures us to the suffering of others, it spawns hypocrisy, it cuts the nerve of action.

Compassion triggers action. And that action is sometimes toward people whose sufferings are so hidden that pity would never be stirred even to feel.

I recently heard of a young white couple (twenty-five or twenty-six years old) who live with their baby in a changing area of Detroit.

A gang of black-jacketed Negro teens was the bane of the neighborhood. They would stretch out across the street so that cars couldn't go through. Sometimes the young couple, along with others, had to turn around and go around the block to get to their apartment or park their car.

The gang did other things equally disconcerting and obnoxious to decent law-abiding citizens.

Last Halloween night the husband went up to the gang, which was standing around on the corner, and said, "My wife and I'd like to invite you to our apartment for a party."

They came.

They had a great time.

And out of that evening came a weekly Bible class in that same apartment. One or two of the teens have become Christians so far.

Judgment and dislike, even hatred—not pity—were the neighborhood's reaction to the teen gang.

Compassion saw the hidden distress that caused the teens' antisocial actions, and compassion planned a party.

Risk? Of course. The same sort of risk the Samaritan took when he stopped to help a man who had been beaten by thieves. (Jesus said "He had compassion.")

Compassion can get you hurt, killed even. Jesus Christ, pinnacle of compassion, was crucified.

But compassion reacts in small, unrisky ways as well as big. It's an attitude of life.

A nurse in a big-city hospital told me about a patient, a Skid Row derelict, who said of a certain doctor, "He's the best doctor here."

The nurse was intrigued by his comment, and wondered

what professional actions or attitudes had given the man such a high opinion of the doctor.

"What makes him so great?" she asked.

"Every time he passes my bed, he tweaks my toe," was the unexpected reply.

Compassion moved the doctor to tweak a toe.

A few years ago, a Christian lady in Philadelphia told me about an elderly mother and her son who lived in a row-house neighborhood.

The mother was paralyzed; the son had given up his struggle to live and just stayed at home and ate. As a result, he weighed so very much that he couldn't stoop over to care for his feet.

Two elderly Christian ladies, sisters, lived next door. They cared for the mother, bathing her and nursing her. But they could do nothing for the son.

Hearing about the situation, a young assistant pastor began to stop at the home. He washed the son's feet and cut his toenails.

"And all the time he was doing it," said the lady who was telling me, "that man cursed the young pastor, used obscene language and heaped all sorts of abuse on him. But this didn't stop him."

Nothing stops compassion.

But self-centeredness keeps it from starting. And the sort of harsh, judgmental, "it serves him right" attitude that seems to characterize many of us in the Church.

We need compassion today, not pity, toward the other race, the other generation (according to Jesus, the Prodigal's father "had compassion on him"), the disadvantaged, the sick, society's derelicts and dropouts.

We need it even more than we need air-conditioning or cushions on the pews. But we'll get them first because they can be bought.

Later, maybe, we can hire a young assistant pastor like that one in Philadelphia.

# Are God's Laws the Same for Jerusalem, Corinth, New York?

**August 1969**

Twenty years ago I heard Dr. Martyn Lloyd-Jones say that 1 Corinthians was the most relevant book of the Bible to contemporary life in the West.

I don't know whether the great Bible expositor and minister of London's Westminster Chapel is still of the same opinion. I do know that I've read the book several times since with that thought at the back of my mind.

One obvious parallel between Corinth and the United States is an obsession with sex, to use Harvard Professor Pitirim Sorokin's judgment, which he also gave about twenty years ago. Both cultures, though separated by two millennia, share the obsession, along with accompanying (or resultant) sexual anarchy.

How should Christians behave during such a period of history? Does God suspend His ordinary laws, does He expect a different standard in Corinth from the one in Jerusalem?

Not according to St. Paul's letter. God's laws for those saved out of but living in a pagan society are the same as His laws for those saved out of orthodox Judaism. The Church is responsible to teach and discipline along moral lines laid down by Jesus Christ in either situation.

Moral law is not bent to the configuration of a culture; it bends God's people within a culture to the shape of His will. Perhaps more precisely, it is the standard by which actions are judged and the Spirit's work is recognized.

How could you recognize a Christian Corinthian? One way was by his sexual purity.

How can you tell a Christian American? One way is by his sexual purity.

But isn't it hard, almost impossible, to maintain one's purity in a sexual cesspool?

Of course it is, and that is why it's such a good test of who really is a Christian in this sort of culture. It takes more than a natural man has to pass such a test. It takes a redeeming work of God.

Most of us would let it go at that in our writing or preaching: "Stay pure," we'd say, "and again I say stay pure. 'Thou shalt not commit adultery.' 'Flee youthful lusts.' 'Abstain from fornication.' The closing hymn is number 175, 'True-Hearted, Whole-Hearted.'"

A few would go a step further, as St. Paul did, and demand that the public sinner be publicly disciplined by the Church (1 Cor. 5).

But the Apostle didn't stop at either of these two injunctions. He gave some practical advice.

He knew the power of the sexual drive in men, Jews or Greeks. He knew that the Corinthian manner of dress, public gossip about sexual orgies, on-the-job jokes overheard by Christians, would all be powerful incitements to lust and sin.

"Stay pure" and "True-Hearted, Whole-Hearted" weren't enough. So he advised people in two different situations, married and single. "You married people," he said, "see that you use God's gift of sex for your mutual satisfaction. If you withhold your body from your partner, don't be surprised if he falls into sin. What you are doing is building a temptation trap for him. God gave you a defense against temptation, use it" (1 Cor. 7:2–6, paraphrased).

What about the single person? A recent book, embraced by most of the evangelical community because it came from the "right" publisher, with recommendation from the "right" people, advises single people (the book is aimed at teens): "If you're going to do wrong, then be sure that you do it in the right way." This means, according to the author, to use birth-control devices for premarital sex.

This was not St. Paul's advice to the single man and woman. "Look," he said, "stay single. Don't think marriage will solve the problem of lust. But if you can't contain yourself, if you can't remain pure in Corinth, then get married. But none of this premarital sex" (1 Cor. 7:8, 9, paraphrased).

I suspect that there are some parents even in the Church today, who are less opposed to premarital sex—provided necessary precautions against pregnancy are taken—than they are to early marriage.

If it's a choice, St. Paul seems to me to say, Christians should encourage early marriage if the alternative is unmarried intercourse.

Not because there is a possibility of having a baby, but because purity is Christian, sexual intercourse outside of marriage is pagan.

# PART TWO

# OUT OF
# MY MIND:
# THE SEVENTIES

# MY MEMORIES OF
# MY FRIEND JOSEPH BAYLY
*by Ken Taylor*

Joe and Mary Lou had many wonderful traditions, and my wife, Margaret, and I had the privilege of participating in one of them. Each New Year's Day we would alternate with Joe and Mary Lou in hosting a New Year's breakfast, attended by whoever of their family and ours was available, plus assorted friends.

These were warm and happy hours of a delicious breakfast and a time of sharing of the Lord's goodness to us during the year past, and our looking forward to serving and praising in the year ahead. Joe's reading of an appropriate Scripture and a prayer time were highlights of this annual event.

One of the great sermons I have heard was from Joe on the holiness of God. It was not only a clearer understanding of theology that he gave us, but the awesome demands of God upon our lives as His children which, as Joe pointed out, are all too frequently overlooked in this day of happy religion. For we too are to be holy in thought and action, and to stay away from soul-smirching sources of contamination bringing not only disappointment to God, but His judgment upon us, whether now or in the future when we stand before the Judgment Seat of Christ.

As an interesting sidelight to the above, Joe went twenty years without becoming a member of our church because of its code against dancing and drinking—which he did not do. As a result, it was not until the mid-1980s when the church revised its stance that Joe became a member and an elder of the church, although during those years his influence on us was profound because of our church leadership's respect for him.

Joe taught an adult Sunday school class for twenty years, which Margaret and I attended with great appreciation because of his practical application of Scripture. His teaching style was to ask controversial questions and make us think! His many years of

"Out of My Mind" columns in *Eternity* magazine indicate this same challenging of superficial Christianity. We had this every Sunday.

How confusing it was to me, and perhaps to Joe too, when five-year-old Danny was in the hospital with a serious illness. Coming from visiting Danny, with a heavy heart because of the life-threatening disease that was taking its toll, Joe was walking along a street and an elderly lady approached him and spoke to him to tell him, "Your son will get well again." Joe did not know her, or how she knew he had a son desperately sick, but hoped it was an angel sent from the Lord to give him this assurance. However Danny died within a few days.

The David C. Cook Publishing Company, of which Joe was the President when the Lord took him home, had not been well thought of by many evangelical churches when Joe came as editorial director. God used him in a wonderful way to revise the entire curricula so that it is now one of the outstanding evangelical Sunday school publishers. What a heritage to leave!

One day my daughter Mary Lee, a high school friend of Joe's son Tim, called me from the college campus where she was studying, to say that Tim was in trouble with his dad. Tim was in his hippie days with shaggy hair and beard and "inattention" to family policies in the home. I don't know the whole story and I never asked, but Joe came to the decision that it would be best for Tim to leave. Mary Lee was calling to ask if her friend Tim could move in with Margaret and me in our empty nest. Since I have always liked and enjoyed Tim, as well as because of Mary Lee's request, it was easy to give Tim the invitation.

He lived with us for several months. A couple years later Joe and I participated in joining Tim and Mary Lee in marriage.

When Joe went to be with the Lord (and with his three sons who preceded him to heaven), Tim told me, weeping, "Now you are the only father I have." No, Tim, I can't replace your father— this practical, godly, wonderful man, my friend Joe Bayly.

—Ken Taylor
Wheaton, Illinois
November, 1992

# The Stumbling Bush

Do beards stumble weaker brothers or gratify stronger sisters?

What happens when a middle-aged man grows a beard?

Last summer I spent two weeks at Inter-Varsity's Colorado camp, Bear Trap Ranch, with Mary Lou and our three sons. Most of the men were combing their faces.

As we pulled out of camp onto the road down Cheyenne Mountain on our way home, Mary Lou said something like, "Why don't you grow a beard?"

That was all the encouragement I needed. From that day to this the jawline of my face has been untouched by a razor. (The style has been variously described as Abe Lincoln or Captain Ahab. I prefer to think of it as my own personal adaptation to Illinois winters. They are cold and one has colds.) After four months, I feel that I'm in a position to analyze some effects of my beard.

To many of my peer group, it seems to be some sort of sinister symbol.

"Why did you grow a beard?"

"Because my wife thought she'd like it on me, and so did I. And we do."

"Why did you really grow it?"

At this point I am tempted to answer what the questioner probably wants to hear me say: I have decided to drop out; I want to identify with the younger generation; I am having a delayed identity problem; I want to show my teen-age son that there's one thing I can do that he can't do; I have begun to doubt my masculinity.

Not that all my peers are clutched, or turn into amateur

psychiatrists. But negative reactions are pretty well limited to my middle-aged contemporaries.

Old people often say, "You know, my father had a beard . . . I like it." And young people couldn't care less. (I think that if they felt I had grown it in an attempt to identify with them, they'd despise me. But they don't, I think.)

You know, I'd never in a hundred years go up to a lady and say, "Why do you wear your hair that way? It looks lousy." But women, some of whom I've hardly met, feel free to comment negatively on my facial hair. One Christian woman, after I had answered her questions (a real inquisition), and assured her that yes, my wife does like my face this way, turned to her husband with a drill-sergeant's look and said, "You grow a beard and I get a divorce."

It's the quiet, feminine woman who's likely to say, "I like your beard."

Now some real ladies say things like, "I wish my husband worked for a company that would tolerate a beard." Or, "My husband grew a beard one summer, but the chairman of his department said the beard went, either without him or with him."

And one lady, on her way out of Sunday school, commented, "A beard is like a picnic. It's more fun when you have to go through the underbrush to get there."

I suspect that the fact that my beard is a different color from my hair is another factor that throws people. One lady wanted to know if I dye my hair; a barber in San Francisco wanted to dye my beard; and someone close to me says it looks as if I've spilt some milk on me.

On a couple of occasions I have received the arm-around-the-shoulder, "Dear Brother" treatment.

One man I respect spent twenty minutes trying to get me to shave. It was a pure labor of love on his part, since I did not work with him. He felt that I was drawing attention to myself by my beard, and that I was trying to identify with the younger generation. My protestations that he was wrong had no weight at all. (And this column will probably convince him that he is right.)

Many men are quiet advocates. "I wish I could grow one" is

fairly often expressed. By this the speaker means either "I can't even grow sideburns," or "My wife/boss/church wouldn't stand for it."

One elderly man shook his head as he told me, "You'll be sorry you ever grew that beard." I thought he meant I'd lose all my friends, or be excommunicated, or something. But he soon cleared that up when I asked why: "Because your skin will get dry and crusty, and it will be raw when you finally shave it off."

So far my skin is in good shape. It may be a bit thicker than it was before.

The ultimate weapon to several who have used it, the one that should end the matter and get me to shave, is not scaly skin, however. It is a prime doctrine of the past thirty years: "Have you considered the weaker brother?" (1 Cor. 8).

"Who is the weaker brother?" I ask, gaining time to think.

"Why, the one who might stumble as a result of your having it."

"You mean my exercising my Christian freedom to have it?"

"Yes. The weaker brother."

"The one who objects, or the one who stumbles?"

"Who might stumble."

"The ladies and men in churches who have come up to me and told me I ought not to have it, or it looks lousy?"

"Yes."

"They're not weaker brothers," I say triumphantly. "I asked one if he was a weaker brother, and he was offended. I'm the weaker brother, and my fellow weaker brothers like my beard. It's the stronger brothers who object."

Last Sunday I discovered a new doctrine that I'd like to see developed during the next thirty years. It's the argument of the stronger sister.

Mary Lou (who represents the *genus*) handed me the December issue of *Woman's Day* soon after I returned home from a trip (on a plane).

"Read what Ruth Bell Graham says about beards," she said. And I read from an interview.

"I've learned that the students with beards [in a college-age Sunday school class she teaches] are usually more interesting. I may not agree with them, but I'm always stimulated. They're original and they have the courage to be different." Ruth reflected a moment before going on. "Beards are really very masculine and I'm all for that. I think it takes a mature man to grow one and a mature woman to appreciate it. I'd even like Bill to grow a beard!"

If there's a stronger sister than Billy Graham's wife (outside my own home), I don't know her.

This year for the first time, I've been honored by being asked to serve as Santa Claus at the company Christmas dinner. Ho, Ho, Ho!

# High Price of TV
## February 1970

As we enter the '70s, psychologists have become our conscience in areas of human behavior. Warnings about the effects of TV-watching are coming from psychiatrists and educators—not from pastors.

The Church has apparently defaulted on its responsibility in favor of the psychologists. Whatever threat pastors see in television is not related to its effect on the human mind and behavior, but the effect on Sunday evening church attendance and pastoral home visitation.

Dr. S. I. Hayakawa, the embattled president of San Francisco State University, points out that by the time a typical American boy or girl has reached the age of eighteen, he or she has had 12,000 to 15,000 hours of TV-viewing. These are not hours stolen from school, but from relating to other people: parents, siblings, neighbors, the elderly, strangers. He concludes that it's small wonder so many students drop out; they did not learn how to get along with other human beings during their formative years.

Dr. Graham Blaine, chief psychiatrist in the student health service of Harvard University, has said that the most serious problem of TV is not poor programming, but that it has destroyed the average family's exchange of views and information at the evening meal. People are anxious to get to a favorite program, he says, and so they hurry to finish eating. What happened during the day, the little things, and bigger matters are never discussed.

When was the last time you heard a preacher or Sunday school teacher warn about the family-fragmenting effects of television?

Is the Church even remotely concerned about what this electronic communications medium is doing, may eventually do, to the human behavior of Christians? I think not. What I hear— when I hear anything—is the soul-destroying effect of the theater in the theater, not the theater in the living room. Movies seem to have a baptism of purification when they are shown on TV.

The daughter of a friend's pastor put it this way: "I can hardly wait till that movie is shown on television, so I can see it."

What will be the long-range effects of TV on the American mind and morals, on the Christian mind and morals?

For perspective on the question, one psychologist says that the average child today, who follows the typical American viewing pattern, will by age sixty-five have spent nine years of twenty-four-hour days sitting in front of a TV set. (If he went to Sunday school every Sunday during those years, he will have spent about four months studying God's Word.)

Even if TV were morally neutral, it would have serious effects on Christian life and thought. You don't spend nine years of life watching anything without being affected by it. Or even six or seven years.

"It's so cute the way our little boy can sing all the commercials." I've heard that statement several times; so have you. But even if it's cute, is it worthwhile? Is such mental conditioning, perhaps, in the long view dangerous?

What view of life do people get from TV? Secular,

materialistic, man-shall-live-by-bread-alone. What view of family life? Fragmented, strong mother, feeble father. What view of human life? Cheap, meaningless, here-and-now, hedonistic. What view of reading? What's a book? What view of God? Who's He, apart from a Billy Graham special?

Do Christian people even think of what Dean Martin, Tiny and Vicki Tim, Johnny Carson do to them and their children? Is this the sort of guest we want to invite into our living rooms every week?

What about family Bible reading? Prayer? If these are missing and Dean Martin, or Rowan and Martin are welcomed, aren't we shouting something to our children and ourselves, something about the real values of life now and hereafter? No Sunday school, or later a Christian college, can replace that value system.

But TV is not morally neutral. It was a secular writer in the *Detroit News* (Kathy Sudomier, a thirty-six-year-old newspaper woman), not a preacher, who screamed loudly enough about TV advertising—"You dirty old ad men make me sick"—to awaken *Advertising Age* to a potential threat.

Has the church yielded its role of moral guidance, along with other roles, to secular society in our time?

After giving examples of sexually arousing pictures and dialogue in TV advertising, Mrs. Sudomier concludes: "If you think this generation represents the New Morality, then look out for the next one, Granddad. You'll have our kids turned into the most over-sexed, over-sated monsters since the fall of the Roman Empire."

A medical doctor in West Germany warned several years ago that the country that once knew the tyranny of Hitler now faces the tyranny of evil. And the United States, which has never—except in localized situations—known totalitarianism, seems to be embracing a tyranny of evil.

In my opinion, this represents an interesting switch on George Orwell's *1984:* It is not Big Brother observing human life in every room by TV cameras who thereby controls life; Big

Brother performs on TV in every room and thereby determines life.

If our Lord Christ returns during the '70s, will He find faith in the United States (Luke 18:8)?

# God or Caesar?

Caesar is posing new threats

**May 1970**

W. C. Fields disliked children. So did George Bernard Shaw.

In *Back to Methuselah,* Shaw wrote about an imaginary, remote future—the result of evolution—in which human beings come out of eggs at about age seventeen, equipped with all they need to know about past culture. Like bees or weaver birds, patterned to find honey or build nests, these humans are fully programmed for mature life. They have no need to follow the procedure that Shaw found so wasteful, of spending decades to stuff their brains with what others have already mastered.

Shaw did not see childhood as a period of wonderment, of curiosity, but as an "awkward, stumbling immaturity."

Children are God's gift to the race (Ps. 127:3). Contrary to Fields and Shaw, the Bible considers them the crown of life, an inheritance from God, the stuff of which heaven is made. And the training of children is the great challenge of fathers and mothers.

"Talk about careers for women," a psychologist said. "What greater career could there be than that of bringing the next generation into existence and civilizing it?"

Not everyone sees it that way.

The contemporary "women's liberation" movement is trying to achieve real equality for this silent co-majority. Writing in the

*Atlantic Monthly*, Catherine Drinker Bowen says, "Perhaps the real turn of the road will come—and I predict it is coming soon—when more than two children to a family will seem bad taste, like wearing mink in a starving village. No woman can devote a life to the rearing of two, she cannot even make a pretense of it. When the mother image loses its sanctity, something will take its place on the altar. . . ."

Since when were two children too few for a woman's *raison d'être?* Is a typewriter or sales counter sufficient to justify the devotion of her life?

That figure of two is the maximum per family our social planners have now established. Prevention of conception and abortion are the prescribed means. Tax incentives or penalties are the initial persuaders.

Pharaoh in Egypt and Hitler in Germany had more advanced persuaders to achieve population control.

I know that we couldn't conceive of our present or future good American rulers using such means.

Or could we?

Is the American human less corrupt than his ancient Egyptian or recent German counterpart?

During the twenties and thirties, one reason our parents were convinced of the evil nature of communism was because Russian mothers turned their little children over to state nursery schools so they could work.

And in the forties we were filled with horror when we learned about German experiments in genetic control, to weed out defective human beings.

Now our country has adopted the earlier Russian pattern, and our scientists are seriously proposing abortion to achieve a goal similar to the Hitlerian one.

I was in an informal discussion of abortion recently. A man skilled in his profession—crippled since birth—was a silent listener. Later he said to me, "On that basis, I would have been destroyed in the womb."

When a sperm cell unites with an egg, the result is a totally different being from the woman who nourishes and protects it for the next nine months. It has individual status at that moment, not four months later.

As John Archibold, Denver Christian lawyer, puts it, abortion is the one example of a human being—albeit a proto-human—who is legally executed without a hearing, without being given the opportunity to defend his right to live.

And if we thus condemn the unborn to death, can we be sure that this will not be the "legal" answer to the defective elderly in another generation?

I am not stupid. Therefore I am aware of the necessity for thought and planning in connection with the impending population crisis.

But the Christian is not coerced by the crisis or government into a position that—to his lights, at least—conflicts with the Bible and Christian doctrine.

Government determination of the number of children my wife shall have is intervention in an area where we are alone with God. Government control of our right to have a child who is less than perfect (in the Hitlerian sense) is the same sort of intervention.

I know a nine-year-old boy who has a congenital problem of the sort that might have been justification for early destruction of the fetus. Yesterday I heard him pray, "Thank You for the beautiful world You have given us. Please keep people from spoiling it."

Mr. Shaw must never have known such a boy. And Mrs. Bowen couldn't have known his mother.

# Raison d'être

What's worth the investment of a woman's lifetime?

In a recent column I questioned the contemporary attitudes of some women toward child-bearing and abortion, and pressures for governmental controls in the areas of birth and eugenics.

Some women wrote to me.

One wanted to know whether I was talking about single women when I asked, "Is a typewriter or sales counter sufficient [reason] to justify the devotion of her life?"

No, that was a question aimed at Catherine Drinker Bowen, whom I quoted in the previous paragraph: "No woman can devote a life to the rearing of two [children], she cannot even make a pretense of it."

God uses many single women, as well as childless women—whether without children, or having children who are no longer dependent on their mother—in a variety of careers. They represent some of the greatest assets in business, medicine, teaching, and in many Christian organizations and missions.

I'm glad for the increased recognition and opportunity women are receiving today: equal pay for equal work, increasing opportunity to compete with men for executive-level positions and professional status.

The American Bible Society recently appointed Ruth Culley to direct its Philadelphia office. Miss Culley also directs the Pennsylvania Bible Society, the first woman to hold these positions. It's hard to say that I commend the Bible Society for this step without appearing to be a condescending male, but I do.

But a woman with children, especially young ones, should not scorn child-training as a career of sufficient magnitude to provide her *raison d'être*. This is my opinion, and I believe it has a biblical basis.

The Christian welcomes some cultural changes, accepts some, rejects some. Our criterion in each decision must be the Bible, if the Bible speaks on the matter. If it does not speak, we are dependent on a Bible-programmed, Spirit-enlightened conscience. And the Spirit may use Christian teachers and the Christian community as one means to that enlightenment.

Another letter came from a woman who wrote about "the main point that is glaringly missing [from my prior column]—the right of a woman to say what will happen to her own body. I have a wonderful Christian husband, several kids of high school age and a six-month-old baby. I cherish him—now. But I pray earnestly that my daughter will live in a time when she will have the ability to decide how many children she will have, and when. No man will ever understand the emotions and physical stress that come to a woman who unwillingly bears a child."

I suppose not. But "emotions and physical stress" are known to the God who made us, to the Christ who redeemed us. And it is He to whom we must answer, whether male or female, for our attitudes and actions.

Do women really have to wait for their daughters' time to "decide how many children to have and when"? Not if we're talking about the control of conception, and that husband is really a "wonderful Christian."

But the decision to abort existing life is not the same as the decision not to conceive life, in my opinion. As a Christian, I consider the new morality of abortion by choice evidence of the post-Christian, pagan nature of our society. (I have no question about aborting in the event of rape, a slight question about aborting when the girl is single, although I am inclined to accept this as well. Perhaps I am inconsistent in my views,* but Old Testament law usually was also fitted to a variety of occasions.)

How often the womb is mentioned in the Bible: "Thou didst knit me together in my mother's womb" (Ps. 139:13); "the Lord who made you, who formed you from the womb" (Isa. 44:2; Job 31:15). Perhaps we Christians need a fresh sense of awe at God's involvement in the creation of a new life through two of His children whom He has brought together, rather than so much light talk of curettage and vasectomy.

Another woman wrote to rebuke me for the fact that I have fathered my own children, instead of raising other people's

---

*Editor's note:* Compare Dad's position here with his later understanding of the abortion issue in the December 1981, June 1984, and January 1986 articles. When asked once why a major evangelical leader of his acquaintance had taken the position reflected above (abortion acceptable in certain extraordinary cases), he answered, "Ignorance."

"unwanted" children. This is her solution to overpop: "voluntary vasectomies—by the millions."

But at the risk of losing those who see things differently, I do not believe adoption is, or should be—in most instances—a substitute for a Christian couple's bringing their own children to birth, and then raising them.

As I understand the Bible, a "goodly heritage" (Ps. 16:6) involves familial lines of descent, not just environment. It seems to me that great stress is laid on ancestors in the Bible, not just on who raises the child.

Therefore I believe the world and the church need more children of Christians, not just more children raised by Christians.

I hasten to add that God delights in taking roots out of a dry ground (Isa. 53:2), and turning them into great giants of trees. From the standpoint of His contemporaries, Jesus was such a root. And God brings the mighty low. So what I have said previously is not to downgrade adopted children. But I hope adopted children who love God will—when they are married—have their own children, rather than limiting themselves to adoption.

But let's not put all our problems into the overpop basket. Writing in the *New Republic,* Ben Wattenberg suggests that over-population is the current scapegoat for various national ills: pollution, depletion of natural resources, poverty. Among the examples he gives is the panic button apocalyptic demographers have punched in connection with our wilderness, that has been vanishing "because of too many people." But in less than twenty years, visits to national parks have gone up by more than 400 percent, while population has increased only 30 percent. So there must be other factors. These factors (in all areas, including poverty) are more difficult to control and program for change than over-population. So this takes the front of the stage.

# *God & the U.S.A.*

Can our circular arguments deliver us
from judgment?

**August 1970**

**M**y favorite spot in Washington, D.C., is the
Lincoln Memorial. I like to visit it at night.

One Sunday night last May, I walked up the long steps in the
warm darkness, and came out into the great open space before that
compassionate white stone, the statue of Mr. Lincoln.

Some oddly garbed students, probably left over from the
previous day's demonstration at the Ellipse, stood silent before the
statue.

On the left-hand wall, carved in stone, is the Gettysburg
Address. I walked over to read it. I remembered how my second
grade teacher didn't believe me when I said that my grandmother
shook hands with President Lincoln after he spoke. But she did;
she was a little girl who lived just outside Gettysburg.

Then I walked to the opposite wall and read his Second
Inaugural Address. The students were there, reading it.

"Woe unto the world because of offenses? for it must
needs be that offenses come; but woe to that man by whom
the offense cometh" [Matthew: 18:7]. If we shall suppose that
American slavery is one of those offenses which, in the
providence of God, must needs come, but which, having
continued through His appointed time, He now wills to
remove, and that He gives to both North and South this
terrible war, as the woe to those by whom the offense came,
shall we discern therein any departure from those divine
attributes which the believers in a living God always ascribe to
Him? Fondly do we hope—fervently do we pray—that this
mighty scourge of war may speedily pass away. Yet, if God

wills that it continue until all the wealth piled by the bondman's two hundred and fifty years of unrequited toil shall be sunk and until every drop of blood drawn with the lash shall be paid with another drawn with the sword, as was said three thousand years ago, so still it must be said, "The judgments of the Lord are true and righteous altogether" [Revelation 16:7].

Disturbing words. More disturbing than yesterday's demonstration. . . . Is God concerned with nations, or only with individuals? Is the state—the United States—subject to moral law?

*Jesus is coming back. The mess our nation is in doesn't concern us Christians. We'll escape all judgment.*

But what if that isn't for two hundred years?

*Look, the Jew is back in Palestine, there are earthquakes all over the place, wars and rumors of wars. It can't be two hundred years.*

What if it is? The Bible is pretty clear that God judges the nations.

*That's Old Testament. And Israel was a theocracy, which the United States isn't.*

A lot of Christians treat our nation's history as if it were. And react as if critics of the government were touching something holy.

*Well, the Apostle Paul in Romans 13 says that "the powers that be are ordained of God" (v. 1). So we ought to realize we're not exactly pleasing God when we criticize our government.*

Does that "powers that be" include all government?

*Of course.*

Russia and China and Poland? Should Christians in those nations accept what their government does as something holy?

*No, because it isn't. It's atheistic.*

Then our government really is a theocracy.

*No. But let's get back to where judgment is found: in the Old Testament. And there God judged His own nation.*

He also judged other nations: Syria and Egypt and Babylon, Edom and city states like Sodom and Gomorrah.

*But we're living in the New Testament age, the age of grace.*

Do you mean that God's different today, that He's gone soft?

Will He let the United State get away with things He didn't let Egypt or Babylon or Sodom and Gomorrah get away with?

*I mean that God deals with individuals today, not nations.*

So the United States really is above God's laws. We Christians can relax whatever happens. Amos isn't profitable to us for doctrine and rebuke. The United States is even better than a theocracy—but what about Rome? Its downfall was after the New Testament was written. And France. Russia.

*Nations fall, even today.*

Even the United States?

*Let's go over to the Jefferson Memorial.*

It's closed for repairs. Sinking into the ground. Do you remember Jefferson's words, "I tremble for my country when I remember that God is just."

*He wasn't a Christian.*

# Verdict: Guilty

... and feelings of shame are not enough

**December 1970**

The spiritual revival at Wheaton College last winter was different from previous revivals during the past thirty-five years.

Students waited their turn at the front of the auditorium to speak as they had before, but what they said was different.

Guilt over wrong conduct—cheating and breaking rules—was almost completely missing. In its place was a revival of relationships.

"It was as if they saw other people for the first time," an old professor commented. In the revival's aftermath, David Howard, Inter-Varsity Christian Fellowship's missionary director, and I noticed the same thing: now students smiled at you on campus, spoke to you, stopped to talk.

I've tentatively concluded that revival today creates a happy—perhaps *joyous* is a better word—student freed to relate to others.

Of course, that's significant in an age where teens and young adults do not find it easy to relate to one another. (A friend of mine who visited a rock festival in the Northwest described what he saw: "Ten thousand individuals, not a group. Everyone was isolated from everyone else.")

*But why no guilt?*

James N. Lapsley, associate professor of pastoral theology at Princeton Theological Seminary, suggests that we are in transition from a guilt-oriented to a shame-oriented culture. In his opinion, this represents the basic cultural revolution which is taking place around us.

> Guilt stems from an apprehension of some code or law violated, written or unwritten, conscious or unconscious. Its core is a sense of "badness," for which one fears punishment. . . . Shame stems from an apprehension of failure, of not measuring up, and the core feeling is weakness, for which one fears that he will be ousted for membership in the community whose standards he has embraced. The root meaning of shame is a covering (to attempt to hide one's shortcomings), while guilt originally referred to something owed, a debt. . . . Shame is always relational, while guilt may not be.*

How do you deal with shame?

In the contemporary youth culture the answer is, you "let it all hang out." You become shameless, you do everything "out front," where everyone can see you.

To be inhibited or uptight is a cardinal sin, according to this way of looking at things, that will result in expulsion from the community.

To demonstrate their triumph over shame, some of today's

---

*The Journal of Pastoral Care

youth shout obscenities during demonstrations and display their nudity at rock festivals. "Everything was see-through," my friend at the festival in the Northwest told me. "Blouses, tents, everything. The people themselves."

\* \* \*

When Adam and Eve sinned, their first reaction was not guilt but shame. And so they covered their nakedness—ineffectively, but covered it nonetheless.

When God intruded on their hideout, He made for them a complete covering. That covering was provided by an innocent animal, sacrificed to take care of guilt as well as shame.

The days of shameless paradise, with its innocent nudity, were past. Guilt and shame had entered the race. Both needed covering.

The Old Testament sacrificial offerings were propitiatory, removing the offense or guilt and taking away the shame.

Likewise, our Lord Jesus Christ's death on the cross was propitiatory (not just expiatory). It was a sacrifice and a covering for sin.

Liberal theology finds this offensive. I remember a comment by Dr. C. T. Craig of Oberlin School of Theology during a summer course at Union Seminary in 1942. Dr. Craig, one of the RSV translators, was explaining the committee's decision at that time to substitute the word *expiation* for *propitiation* in Romans 3: "Any attempt to show that there was something in the essential nature of God that demanded satisfaction for sin ends only in blackening the character of God."

But, Dr. Craig not withstanding, there was, and there is. God's holiness and man's guilt are biblically substantiated facts, whether they are popular contemporary conceptions or not.

I think it will become more and more difficult to get through to people with biblical theology. Maybe it is impossible in the general youth culture, but we must with our own youth. The answer to our Lord Christ's question, "When the Son of man returns, will he find faith on earth?" (Luke 18:8) may be at stake.

# Wrong Fences

How false landmarks can lead to disaster

**January 1971**

In a lecture at Haverford College several weeks ago, Dr. Kenneth Boulding, noted economist, gave a mind-stimulating view of the world.

The world, Dr. Boulding said, makes him think of a mesa, one of those high plateaus with precipitous sides that are found in the Southwest.

Fences are necessary at the mesa's edge to keep people from stepping off to destruction. We all recognize the need for such fences.

But some people build fences in other parts of the mesa, places where there's no danger. These fences are not merely unnecessary; they are dangerous.

The unnecessary fence is dangerous because people who manage to breach it without injury and who then only find more of the mesa beyond the fence are likely to conclude that all fences are extraneous—including those vital ones that guard against the precipice.

But we have not been satisfied with the fences God erects in the Bible: fences of morality and ethics, justice and righteousness. We had to get in the fence-building business ourselves.

We've spent fifty years cluttering up the mesa with fences. And we've given these manmade fences the same coat of authoritative paint as biblical ones, the "thus saith the Lord" ones.

There's a fence against a white person marrying a black person, a fence against movie-going, against fellowship with true Christians who belong to the wrong church council, a fence against cosmetics and hair and music, a fence against various political, social and economic systems.

We've been a generation of fence-builders, of mesa-dividers.

Now our children come along and breach the fences we've built so carefully, located so logically. They breach them and find that nothing happens.

So they come to scorn fences. They lump all fences together, God's and ours, and will have none of them.

"The mesa has no danger, see, we've gone through the fences with impunity"—until they face the precipice.

Has your heart ached for a Christian girl who had a baby out of marriage, a Christian boy who shacked up with a girl without marriage, a young person on drugs, a teen who became involved in shop-lifting, a Christian man who marries a non-Christian woman, a Christian couple who slide into divorce and remarriage?

The list is heartbreakingly long. And I guess I've concentrated too heavily on the sex-oriented ones; it's easy in our American culture. But the point is our fences divert attention from God's fences. Sometimes, I am tempted to think we locate them where we do with this in mind. We build a fence against the inter-marriage of white and black so that the warning of God's Word against sub-Christian attitudes toward the stranger and the poor are obscured. Our fence of patriotism hides the fence Jesus Christ erected against yielding to Caesar the Christian conscience that forever belongs to God.

We see these fences of God so clearly in another culture, another age.

We recognize that Shinto-shrine worship was patriotic but wrong for Christians in pre-World War II Japan and that persecution of the Jews was patriotic but wrong for Christians in Hitler's Germany.

But for Christians in the United States, are there no parallels? Has God given us the privilege of living in the first "Christian" state in history? If we think this is so, we may be in danger of totally yielding our conscience to the judgments of our rulers.

God's fence is still there. Our manmade fences may hide it, but it remains. And it judges us if we allow the American flag to become our Shinto shrine, the black our Jew.

Let's tear down our fences so that we may get a fresh view of God's fences. Then maybe our young will begin to run from the edge of the precipice.

# Pharisaism in Retrospect

A letter written over a century ago helps us see evangelical prejudice in perspective. Is this spirit with us still?

**May 1971**

The letter that follows could probably have been written in any century to any organization or denomination of the Christian church.

Actually, it was written to an interdenominational organization in the middle of the nineteenth century—an organization that survived the subsequent Civil War and is still with us in evangelical strength. I include the name for historical accuracy, not to imply that this particular organization was alone then—or now—in its course of action.

*To Rev. R. S. Cook*
*Corresponding Secretary*
*American Tract Society*

Reverend Sir: I have been favored with your letter of the last month, setting forth the pecuniary exigencies of the American Tract Society, and suggesting to my "charitable consideration" a donation to its funds. Few persons hailed with more satisfaction than myself the establishment of your Society, or more cordially approved the truly catholic principles on which it was founded. I long since became one of its Life Directors, and have frequently contributed to its funds. The professed object of the Society was to inculcate Christian faith and practice, and to a very great extent it has been faithful to its profession, and I doubt not that it has been largely instrumental in promoting the spiritual welfare of multitudes. . . .

About a year since, the ministers and delegates of the Congregational Union of Fox River, Illinois, addressed a very Christian letter to the Society. In this letter they forcibly remarked: "We feel sure that the time has come when the continued absence from the publications of your Society of all that relates to slavery will be significant; that silence can no longer be neutrality or indifference; and that a tract-literature which speaks less plainly of slavery than of other specific evils will conduce to a defective, partial, and unsound morality."

In your official reply of 27th February, 1852, without letting a word escape your pen acknowledging the sinfulness of American slavery, you urge various reasons for not breaking the silence so long observed by the Society respecting human bondage. "It would seem a sacrifice of a greater to a lesser good to engage in the discussion of a topic already exhausted, with the likelihood of satisfying none, and with the certainty of alienating multitudes of our best friends," etc. Your publications, we are informed, must be of a character "calculated to meet the approbation of all evangelical Christians," and you seem to think that, amid the anti-slavery agitation, it is desirable "that at least one institution should move forward on the simple errand that brought the Savior into the world—proclaiming Christ and him crucified," etc.; and you aver that "on no subject, probably, are evangelical Christians more at variance" than slavery; and you conclude with declaring that "the course of duty seems plain before us to adhere as a Society to the simple Gospel in its essential saving truths."

I am unable to reconcile the position assumed in your letter with the past action of the Society, or with the usually received ideas of Christian obligation.

As far as I can judge, the publications of your Society have been in accordance with the rule you announce on no other subject whatever, except human bondage. You suspend the proclamation of "Christ and him crucified," to rebuke Christians for mingling in the dance, or witnessing feats of horsemanship in the circus; but you can spare no time to talk about the sin of robbing black men of every civil and religious right, of scourging men, women and children at pleasure, and of driving them in chained coffles from one market to another.

It is no impiety, it seems, to turn for a while from the contemplation of the crucified Redeemer, to expatiate on the sin of selling and drinking wine and rum; but very far from your Society is the thought of wasting a moment on the traffic in husbands, wives, and children. . . .

Your Committee tells us, in their last report, that they "have never lost sight of their responsibilities to those of tender years," [yet] the Committee knows that in some of our states even a free mother, if her complexion be dark, is by law liable to be scourged on her bare back, should she be caught teaching her little ones to read your Child's Paper; yet not a word of remonstrance escapes the American Tract Society!

In the very last number of *The Child's Paper* I read that there are "between 10,000 and 12,000 children in the city of New York who never enter a church or school, and who can not read the Bible. Here are heathen at home; what is being done for them? These children must be cared for."

Indeed! And is it nothing to your Society that there are in our country about half a million little black heathen who are prevented by law from reading the Bible? These little heathen have souls as imperishable, destinies as momentous, as the white heathen in New York. Must this half million be cared for? Ah! that is a "point of disagreement among evangelical Christians" and hence the Society must not even recognize the existence of children who do not belong to their parents. . . .

It is not desired by any that your institution should be converted into an anti-slavery any more than into an anti-gambling Tract Society. All that is asked is, that this great and influential Christian association should publicly dissent from the impious claim made by the advocates of American slavery, that this vast mass of accumulated sin and misery is sanctioned by the God of

mercy and justice, and allowed by the crucified Redeemer; in other words, that American slavery should share in the condemnation you bestow on "the theatre, the circus, and the horse-race."
(Signed) William Jay
New York City

Jesus said, "But woe to you Pharisees! for you tithe mint and rue and every herb, and neglect justice and the love of God; these you ought to have done, without neglecting the others" (Matt. 23:23).

We are heirs of the Pharisees' herb gardens.*

# Reflections on a Starlit Night

An evening in Brazil gives a poignant
new perspective

## December 1971

Caxambu, Brazil.

We leave the missionary meeting before it's over, four of us, and decide to see the town.

It is dark as we climb the hill to a lighted building. But moon and stars shine clearly.

"That's a school," one of the men says. "They must be having evening classes."

"Let's stop in," I suggest. "I've never seen a Brazilian school."

We arrive just as classes break and are surrounded by students, all young adults. They explain that the school teaches

_Editor's note:_ Shortly before his death, Dad sent me an article written by the then-president of Wheaton College explaining why Wheaton wasn't going to take an official position on abortion. With his fountain pen Dad had scrawled across the top of the page, "Can you imagine Jonathan Blanchard writing this about slavery?"

119

accounting, typing, and other business subjects for people who work during the day. There is a course in English. Some of the students practice on me, then lead us to their teacher.

When he finds that I have just come from the United States, the professor addresses me in formal greeting, telling me that he and his people appreciate America's leadership in this present period of history.

I reply that I appreciate Brazil, and that my three friends, and other missionaries, have told me a lot about Brazil's greatness.

He then suggests that we all have coffee, and so we move to the center court where there is an urn. (Many Latin American schools are built around a patio, with concrete or stone surface and tropical plants. Classrooms surround the patio.)

Brazilian coffee is served in small cups, smaller than demitasse, and is very strong. At first I tried drinking it without sugar— the way I like it—but soon gave up. When I began to pile the sugar in, I began to enjoy it. ("You just have to look at it as a different drink from coffee," one missionary told me.)

We are joined at the patio by another teacher—accounting—who, I'm told, is the mayor of the town. My three friends are engaged in animated conversation with students.

"The mayor wants to know where you come from in the United States," the English professor says.

"Chicago," I reply.

Surprisingly, to me, the name draws a blank from the mayor.

"Chicago," I repeat.

Again, no response.

So I point my index finger at him like a gun barrel, and say, "Bang-bang."

Now he understands: "Ah, Texas!" he shouts with a total smile.

The mayor now has an idea. "He wants to show you and your friends the town of Caxambu," I'm told. "He has a car."

This sounds great until we see the car: a VW beetle. And all four of us are big men.

"We'll walk," someone suggests, but the mayor will have none of it. He settles three of us in the back seat, then, as he gets in the driver's seat—slaps the top of the car. He says something in Portuguese that has the three missionaries laughing.

"What did he say?" I ask.

" 'Volkswagen: not much of a body, but the soul of a woman!' "

After showing us the market area, and some residences, the mayor drives up a steep hill on a winding road. At the top, he gets out to open a gate through the barbed-wire fence, and the car is surrounded by curious cattle.

"Now you shall see our cathedral," he says with pride.

We walk to the edge of the small flat area, and come to an overhang. Below us in the valley, and across on another hill, are pale outlines of houses in the moonlight. Some—not many because it is now ten o'clock—have lights that shine through windows and doors. Above us is the moon—the same moon that looks down on my home in Illinois, and that Americans have walked on.

The mayor's words, soon translated, interrupt my appreciation of beauty above and across and below.

"You must face the other way," he says. "The cathedral is there."

We turn to see the vaulted stone building. It is impressive in the night's pale light. One lamp flickers through a window.

"The sister of our great emperor, Dom Pedro, built the cathedral more than a century ago," the mayor explains. "She had been barren for some years of her marriage until one day she visited our town. After drinking the mineral water here, she went back to her home in Sao Paulo and there conceived. When her baby was born, she was so happy that she traveled back here and announced that she was going to build a cathedral in appreciation for the great gift Caxambu had given her. This, my friends, is her gift."

A cathedral for a baby.

"But we must go. Before we do, I want to show you one other place of interest."

He leads us around to the back of the cathedral, to a low white building. "This is Caxambu's obstetrical clinic."

An elderly, radiant nun answers his knock. After he has introduced her to us as the head nurse, the mayor asks, "How is the little girl I brought in this morning?"

"She has had her baby, by cesarean section. But I don't think she's even aware of what happened."

The mayor turns to us, "Mentally retarded. About twelve years old. My wife and I were awakened by her cries of pain early this morning. She is unknown to us—from the country. Probably someone directed her to our house because I am the mayor of Caxambu. She could not understand her pains, but we realized that they were of childbirth, so I brought her here. Some man violated her."

We squeeze back into the car. The mayor shoos the cattle away, opens the gate, drives through, closes the gate, and we go back down the hill to our comfortable hotel.

# *Is This What Women Want?*

## July 1972

*Social distinctions between men and women go all the way back to creation; contemporary legislative acts can't change them.*

Those of us who acknowledge the Lordship of Jesus Christ, and want to live under His control in this American democracy, believe in equal rights for all. But what are we to make of the Equal Rights (for women) Amendment to the United States Constitution now before the States for ratification? The actual wording of this amendment is: "Equality of rights under the law shall not be denied or abridged by the United States or by any State on account of sex."

I believe that Christian men and women should vote against

ratification. Before you accuse me of male chauvinism, read what a woman, probably not a Christian, says about it: "This does not mean just equal pay for equal work, nor the right to belly up to the bar in the tavern of your choice. It goes far beyond this. Its purpose and effect will be to destroy forever the right of Congress and the fifty State Legislatures to pass any law that differentiates in any way between males and females. As Professor Philip Kurland of the University of Chicago Law School stated, it is 'a demand for unisex by Constitutional mandate.'"

But differences in man and woman, from Creation, are not suddenly erased by a change in personal lifestyles or by legislative act in the twilight of the twentieth century.

Now, objection to unisex doesn't mean that men and women can't wear the same types of clothing or have similar hairstyles. Men and women wore the same kind of long garments in biblical times, and men's hair—although not as long as women's (according to the Apostle Paul)—was not short.

Nor does my objection to ERA mean that I'm against women's receiving the same pay as men for the same job. This is a simple matter of justice. (Constitutional authorities agree that the removal of unjust and unfair discrimination against women is being carried out already under the "equal protection" clause of the 15th Amendment, through Title VII of the 1964 Civil Rights Act.)

I object to unisex and the Equal Rights Amendment because it means that all social distinctions between men and women will be erased. Under ERA women will have to serve in the armed forces along with men. According to an authoritative definitive analysis of ERA in the *Yale Law Journal*, "A woman will register for the draft at age eighteen, as a man now does. . . . Women will serve in all kinds of units, and they will be eligible for combat duty. . . ."

ERA will cause changes in the criminal laws that now protect women. According to the same interpretation of ERA in the *Yale Law Journal:* "The Equal Rights Amendment would not permit such laws [seduction laws, statutory rape laws, prostitution and 'manifest danger' laws], which base their sex discriminatory classification on social stereotypes . . . [even though] the singling out of women [for special protection from sexual coercion] probably reflects sociological reality. . . ." Protective labor laws would also be ended if ERA is ratified.

Is all this what women want? Is it what men want for women? Women are being asked to give up more than they stand to gain for the sake of "equal rights." The biggest thing they will give up is their womanhood.

God didn't make woman to be a sex object. But he didn't make her to be an infantry soldier or tank driver either. He made her to bring the next generation into existence and civilize it, not destroy it. And He made her to keep the present generation from hurtling into hell, through intellect and creativity, spiritual concern and emotion, love and courage.

# *Who Cares About Tomorrow?*
## October 1972

*The current religious scene is blessed with the Jesus movement, the charismatic renewal, and soaring interest in prophecy—or is it?*

W e were discussing King Hezekiah in our Sunday school class. He ruled over Judah, you remember, and ruled well, from the time when he was twenty-five years old.

Then, when he was thirty-nine, Hezekiah faced a personal crisis: he became seriously ill. God told him through His prophet Isaiah, to set his affairs in order for he would soon die.

"Then Hezekiah turned his face to the wall, and prayed to the Lord, saying, 'Remember now, O Lord, I beseech thee, how I have walked before thee in faithfulness and with a whole heart, and have done what is good in thy sight. And Hezekiah wept bitterly" (2 Kings 20:3; Isa. 38:3 RSV).

A natural reaction. The late Philip Howard, Jr., once wrote that a night of pain can do more to cast us on God than many years of ordinary living.

God heard Hezekiah's prayer, saw his tears, healed him and promised to add fifteen years to his life.

Later, when Hezekiah was still living in the glow of health restored, Isaiah came to him with another message from God. This one was for the kingdom, not for Hezekiah personally. The days would come, said God, when the treasures of Judah would be lost to an invading foreign power, when the young men, including Hezekiah's own sons, would be carried captive to Babylon, castrated, and forced into service as slaves.

What was the response of this king who had wept bitterly and cried out to God for mercy in the face of his own impending death?

"Then said Hezekiah to Isaiah, 'The word of the Lord which you have spoken is good.' For he thought, 'There will be peace and security in my days" (2 Kings 20:19; Isa. 39:8 RSV).

What was Hezekiah saying? "I don't care what happens to the next generation, what happens to my children, as long as there is peace in my time. Am I the next generation's keeper?"

I hear the echo of Hezekiah's words today. It is present in politics: "Forget the future, winning the election is all that counts." But I am most concerned about it in the church.

A year ago, I sat next to Editor Russell Hitt at a Christian convention banquet. The speaker was aware of grave problems facing the world; he described them in Doomsday terms. His answer? "Thank God we don't have to face them. Christ is going to return!"

Russ leaned over to me and said, "Do you have the feeling that we went through this once before, thirty or forty years ago?"

Along with Russ Hitt, I see signs of the sort of self-centered isolationism—spiritual isolationism—in the evangelical church today that characterized it in the near past. I see us not merely avoiding the problems raised by *Future Shock, Limits to Growth,* and similar books; I see us retreating from the moral responsibilities we were in the process of accepting a few years ago, in areas such as race and poverty.

My ultimate hope, both personal and social—my only hope—is the return of Jesus Christ. But what if His return isn't in the next five years, what if He doesn't return for seventy-five years, five hundred years?

The Second Coming was never intended to be a cop-out. Nor was the Spirit's work.

I may thank God for spiritual gifts including tongues and healing. But if a personal emotional high, if a reported lengthening of a leg in West Chicago, if the reported turning of water to wine in Indonesia, so possess me that I become ecstatic, while the dreary, frightening prospect of the next generation leaves me cold; if I say, "So be it, just as long as I have God's blessing and God's gifts in my time"—I am sub-Christian.

Our daughter, Deborah, teaches in a Chicago inner-city school. Several months ago she repeated a black thirteen-year-old girl's question, and the question has run through my mind again and again: "How can I get out of the ghetto?"

The Christian answer to that child's question—what is it?

Certainly it is not to retreat to a chamber or stand up in a church meeting and speak in tongues. Nor is it a theologically sophisticated defense of the pre-tribulation (or post-tribulation) rapture.

If Jesus Christ will not return for seventy-five years, or five hundred years, do we have any responsibility to children in the ghetto? (I doubt that Robert Raikes would ever have started the Sunday school for oppressed British children in the late eighteenth century if he had been into tongues and eschatology.) Do we have responsibility for the environment? Do we want present downward trends in politics and government—especially in areas of freedom and morality—projected into the lifetime of our grandchildren?

Can we see fifty years down the road, with total government implementation of B. F. Skinner's philosophy? Do you feel a chill today, as I do, when you learn that the Justice Department has made grants to research the control of occasionally violent people by neurosurgery?

What is a Christian's responsibility? Here are some suggestions:

(1) Be an Isaiah rather than a Hezekiah. Be plugged into God; let others build their empires.

(2) Recognize the enemy, outside and inside. Especially inside.

(3) Let your heart be broken—enough to weep over tragedies not your own. Be moved with compassion.

(4) Keep things in perspective. And the standard of perspective is the whole Bible—Amos as well as Revelation, loving justice as well as charisma.

(5) Find your deepest satisfaction in God and His attributes—rather than in a spiritual high.

# *Women's Lib and the Bible*
## November 1972

My recent column on the proposed Equal Rights (for women) Amendment to the United States Constitution evoked letters in favor of pacifism. Every woman who responded to the column singled out my objection to women in military combat duty, rather than the other effects of the amendment I had noted.

The argument goes like this: "If it's wrong for women to drive tanks and get killed in war, why is it right for men? Women's Lib forces us to reexamine the war." "The fact is that God did not intend that anyone should be a soldier to destroy anything."

Quite obviously, I don't believe God originally created man to destroy. Satan is the destroyer, and by his temptation our first parents fell. Sin entered the race, and with sin the necessity for policemen and soldiers. Sin and policemen and soldiers will cease with the millennium, or with the new heavens and new earth, but not before. Women's Lib cannot hasten or delay the millennium.

The Old Testament is embarrassing to pacifists who claim to believe in its inspiration, because it does not merely say that God permitted war; it says that He commanded it and used it to right wrong, correct injustice, and destroy His enemies. And He commanded His people to fight.

I know that many of my fellow Christians are pacifists because of Jesus' teachings, and I respect their position. Yet there is no record of Jesus or the Apostles commanding a soldier to forsake his military career. And a key Pauline illustration of the Christian life is based on soldiers at war (Eph. 6:10–17). (Can you imagine one based on stealing or prostitution?)

I do not believe God has given carte blanche approval to war, including American wars. One big problem with contemporary Christians is our inclination to sing "The Star-Spangled Banner" to the tune of the "Doxology." In my opinion, this "laboratory of death" (a phrase I heard in Mexico recently) we are perpetuating is quite different from World War II. Sometimes I am sobered by the possibility that I may be standing with German Christians who were silent in the face of Hitler's attempt to exterminate the Jews.

But my point here isn't whether war is right or wrong, whether the Vietnam War is right or wrong, whether Christian participation in war or the Vietnam War is right or wrong. I am rather speaking about the necessity of our having biblical authority for what we believe about war or Women's Lib or anything else.

I was recently at a conference where a distinguished liberal theologian rejected certain teachings of St. Paul on the grounds that he was an arrogant old bachelor and what he said wasn't the Word of God.

I disagreed, but I disagree just as deeply with those who claim to believe in the Holy Spirit's inspiration of the Bible, including the Epistles of Paul but who then proceed to say or imply that we can disregard what he said about the relationship between men and women.

Women's Lib, the ordination of women to the gospel ministry, women's participation in war, the whole concept of unisex, and every other part of the present rethinking of women's role in society and the Church: All are subject and subordinate to the Bible's teaching. Christians start with the Bible, not with Gloria Steinem or Hugh Hefner.

Writing about women's place in the Church, Paul roots it in Creation principles (before the Fall). "I suffer not a woman to teach, nor to usurp authority over the man, but to be in silence. For Adam was first formed, then Eve. And Adam was not deceived, but the woman being deceived was in the transgression" (1 Tim. 2:12–14).

You can rationalize that statement and other statements about the relationship between man and woman that are made in the Bible. You can scorn the Bible's description of male and female roles, husband and wife roles, mother and father roles.

If you do, admit that you've been liberated from the Bible's authority.

On the other hand, if you think the Bible is still true and relevant in this area, why don't you say something, or write something, that reflects your belief? Just make sure that what you say takes into account everything the Bible says, including those statements that Women's Lib ignores or rejects.

# *How Shall We Remember John?*
## May 1973

My big brother John and I were great pals. In fact, our whole family was close, including Mom and Dad, my sister, the brother I'm telling you about, and me. We were close in a way that you find in few families today.

Breakfast was always a special time. We sat around this round oak table with a red-checked cloth on it. Mom almost always served the same thing: steaming hot oatmeal with brown sugar cooked in it (we piled a lot more on top of it too), and milk. A big white pitcher full of milk.

We'd talk about what we were going to do that day, and maybe we'd joke some. Not that we had a lot of time—we didn't, but we had enough to talk some before Dad went off to work and us kids went to school.

John and I were two grades apart in school. That was sort of hard on me, because the teachers who had had him were always comparing us when I got into their class. And the comparison wasn't too flattering to me.

Don't get me wrong. John wasn't a teacher's pet or bookworm. He was a regular guy, and the kids all liked him, including the girls. Maybe one guy who was sort of a bully didn't, but everyone else did.

Life went on like that—breakfast of oatmeal and milk, walk to school, classes, walk home, chores, supper, study around the kitchen table—and you never thought about anything else. Except vacation. Vacation was always stuck in your mind.

You know the kind of life, day after day when it's so great you hope it never ends. Maybe you cry at night sometimes if you ever think of your Mom or Dad dying—you know they will someday. But then you go to sleep, next to John, who's already sawing wood.

It was Christmas vacation, when I was in sixth grade and John was in eighth, that it all suddenly came to an end. Actually, it was two days after Christmas.

John and I had gone to ice skate on Big Pond. It was a real cold day, cold enough so that your scarf got ice on it from your breath. I put on my skates in a hurry and sailed out to the middle of the pond.

I thought I noticed a slight cracking sound from the ice, but it wasn't much and I wasn't worried. It had been pretty cold for about a week. So I showed off some for John, who was still lacing up his skates, sitting on a log, and then I headed for the opposite shore.

John stood up and went real fast right out to the middle too. Just as he got there, I heard this sickening cracking noise, the ice broke up, and John fell through.

I got a long branch and went out as far as I could on the ice. But I couldn't see John anywhere. He had just disappeared. I yelled for him, and I went even farther out, but he just wasn't there.

I must have panicked, because first thing I knew I was running into the house shouting for Mom, crying my eyes out, yelling that John was in the pond. It was awful.

They found his body later that afternoon.

A few days after his funeral, we were sitting at the table, eating breakfast one morning. Nobody was saying anything, but all of us were thinking about that empty chair over against the wall.

You could tell Mom was trying to talk. Finally she just sort of blurted out, "Look, we all miss John, terribly. We loved—love him, and we'll always miss him. Now I have a suggestion to make. Do you remember how he liked oatmeal and milk?"

"Do I!" I said. "I sure do. He used to pile on the brown sugar until . . ."

"That's enough. He liked his oatmeal sweet and so do you. What I want to suggest is this. Let's think about John every time we eat breakfast. Let's remember him whenever we eat oatmeal and drink milk. Let's talk about him . . . ?"

"Yeah, like the time he and I went swimming in Big Pond and . . ." I knew before Dad spoke that I had said something I shouldn't have. Everyone was sort of choked up.

"Time for school," he said. "We can continue this later."

Well, we did. And we agreed with Mom's suggestion. So each morning, when that big pitcher of cold milk went on the table, and our bowls of steaming oatmeal were set in front of us, we'd talk about John.

It wasn't sad talk, but happy. Remembering. I don't mean we never said anything that made us choke up—other people besides me did. But mainly it was happy talk. and we still talked about what we were going to do that day, and even—after awhile—joked some.

One day, some months later, Mom said, "You know, I don't think what we're doing is quite respectful enough for John's memory."

"Respectful?" I said. "Why it's fun. Sometimes it's almost like John is here with us. I like it."

"So do I," Mom said. "But I think we're too casual about it. So I think we ought to set aside a time when we're not rushed like we are at breakfast. Let's say Saturday morning. And we'll remember John in a more fitting place than the kitchen. We'll sit in the parlor, and we'll have a special time worthy of John's memory."

"Aw, Mom," I said. "John always liked breakfast in the kitchen. Lots of oatmeal with plenty of brown sugar on it. And milk. Why make a big deal out of it?"

"That's enough, son," Dad said. "We'll do as your Mother says."

So every Saturday morning, after we had eaten our regular breakfast in the kitchen, we went into the parlor and remembered John.

Mom had gotten some little silver cups for the milk, and some tiny teaspoons for the oatmeal.

Later we only went into the parlor once a month, instead of every week, and now we only do it every three months. It doesn't seem right to me, but I'll soon be leaving home so it doesn't much matter.

I still wish we had never begun that "fitting" remembrance, and had just kept on remembering John every time we ate breakfast.

# *If We Could Rewrite the Bible*

## December 1973

*When you stop to think about it, there are a lot of improvements we could introduce to make a better case for our cherished ideas.*

I was listening to Eugene Chamberlain, coordinator of the children's section of Southern Baptist Sunday School Board, as he explained some difficulties in writing curriculum materials especially telling the Bible story—for children.

"It's hard to maintain suspense," he said, "because you can't whomp a different ending on it."

Suppose we could write Bible stories differently, I thought. What changes, what surprise endings, would we be likely to introduce?

In today's charismatic climate, we'd hardly have St. Paul take a medical doctor with him on his journeys. Luke would be left behind, to carry on his practice among the pagans.

Neither would Paul leave Trophimus behind, sick, at Miletus. A word from Paul, faith on Trophimus's part, would have healed him and restored him to the ministry.

And we'd probably remove Paul's thorn in the flesh.

We'd save lots of people from premature death: John the Baptist, Stephen, maybe even Jonathan. Samson would work his way out of the shambles of Dagon's temple, his sight restored by the shock of falling pillars, and serve God to a ripe old age instead of meeting a tragic end.

Some people would die sooner. Ahab and Jezebel, for instance, and Saul. Why should he have been permitted to hound David all those years and delay David's wonderful kingdom?

We could probably use some people's time and talents to greater advantage. How can you explain the one godly man of his day, Noah, spending years in the shipbuilding business? Wouldn't it have been more appropriate for him to travel around preaching the love of God, or the Quadruple Torah? Maybe, if he had done that, the Flood wouldn't have been necessary.

I guess we'd let the life of Jesus stand as it is, except we might have Him start His public ministry at the age of twenty instead of thirty. Of all men to spend most of His life as a carpenter, He's the last one you'd expect.

We might change a few of His teachings, if it were possible. After all, He was pretty tough on rich people—the camel and the needle's eye, and the rich man who died and was told that he had had his good things on earth. And we'd probably bring Jesus' account of future separation between sheep and goats more into line with Paul's teaching. Jesus' knowing people, and admitting them to heaven, on the basis of their visiting prisoners, clothing the naked, feeding the poor? That sounds a little like salvation by works.

I've always felt sort of sorry for Eli. He seems to have done a good job of raising Samuel, but his own sons were such a mess. Why not make his sons excel him in spiritual vigor and devotion? That would be much more encouraging to us parents today.

At the same time, Eli wouldn't have been overweight.

There's all that wine in the Bible that could be changed to water, or grape juice. And Paul could have advised Timothy to take Maalox, or pray over his upset stomach.

We would surely do something to clean up the violence in the Old Testament, including spikes through foreheads, cutting off big toes, and daggers embedded in fat flesh. And all those battles God's people fought at His command—surely we could find an easier way, and a more moral one, for them to obtain the Promised Land.

One incident, at least, could be changed so that world affairs 4000 years later would be vastly improved. That's the brief affair Abraham had with Hagar, which need never have happened.

Or if it did, she could have aborted.

How about Jacob and Esau? Jacob was such a worm, and

Esau was such a man's man. He must have had charisma beyond Jacob's, so let's make him a leader.

Another turn-around could be Joseph and Potiphar's wife. Why should he go to prison, when he was innocent, while she was free to seduce the next houseboy who came along?

Women: the word conjures up scores of changes we could make in the Bible. The most obvious is to introduce some women among the twelve disciples. Then there's Paul, who could keep his ideas to himself.

A bit more organization of ideas would help in the Bible. It would be great if at least one book were organized as a systematic theology.

And Revelation could be less vague, more specific, like eschatological books today.

When you get right down to it, there are only two incidents you'd really have to change to affect the whole thing: the rebellion of Satan and the fall of man. Those are the ones I'd really like to whomp a different ending on.

# Revise Our "Sexist" Scriptures?

Target of Christian revisionists

**September 1974**

A recent news release indicates that the Revised Standard Version is to be revised yet once more, this time to eliminate sexist language.

What is sexist language? "Sons of God," which will become "children of God." "If any man thirst," which will be changed to "If any person thirst." "He who endures to the end will be saved" will be either "He or she," or "They."

I happen to think the whole idea is stupid, the sort of

135

tampering with the Scriptures that Bible-burners accused the RSV translators of twenty-five years ago.

Before persons begin to write letters accusing me of being a M.C.P., please listen to me say that I think women have a valid and serious cause for complaint in our present American society. I'm for gymnasiums at Christian colleges for women as well as men, equal sports facilities and equipment at Christian camps, women on boards of directors of Christian organizations, equal pay for women for the same work—in Christian as well as secular situations, opportunity for women to advance along with men to executive positions.

And a lot of other things, more basic.

If a woman works all day at employment outside the home, elemental justice would indicate that her husband should share the work of the home.

No husband should be content to flower while his wife vegetates. Every Christian married man is responsible to see that his wife realizes the potential God has built into her life.

But it's not just husbands who must free women to be themselves, to achieve the goals they'd like to achieve. Women's libbers (including many of the Christian ones) need to learn the same lesson. Their scornful put-down of interest in motherhood, in providing a warm and beautiful home, in being a "traditional" wife and mother—forcing a contented wife and mother into a "meaningful career" outside the home, or imposing guilt—is as destructive to many women's freedom as a husband who thinks his wife only exists to further his goals.

Now back to the Bible.

Up to the present time, men have pretty well known who they were, and women have known who they were. There were clear distinctions, both in the Bible and in the general culture.

Nobody felt the need of unisex or bisexuality. In fact, the Bible clearly warned against blurring the lines between the sexes.

Now Germaine Greer and Gloria Steinem come along, and part of the Christian community begins to feel guilty that we are not keeping up with the world. So revisionists take over the Bible and set to work to change it. (I have intentionally chosen a pejorative word; Christian revisionists are comparable to communist revisionist, in my opinion. Both represent an attempt to rewrite history for their own purposes, and tamper with source material.)

Some of the changes—such as the ones I suggested in the second paragraph—aren't too important although I think it's stupid to change a grammatical usage, such as the generic "man." We need a term such as mankind; "chairperson" may be all right, but "personkind" is flawed, in my opinion.

But where will the revisionists stop? Will Adam come from Eve's rib, the serpent tempt Adam, Sarah lead the pilgrimage out of Ur and have a daughter by Abraham's servant, Mrs. Hosea track down a male prostitute husband, Jesus have six women along with six men disciples, Paul travel with a woman doctor? Will the prodigal son become the prodigal daughter (or person)?

Granted that we have stressed God's maleness too much (He is compared to a mother in Scripture, as well as a father), but does the Incarnate Son become a Daughter? Do we erase the Creation-based, not Fall-based, distinction St. Paul makes in 1 Corinthians 11?

When you start to rewrite history, you're in trouble, whether it's communist history or biblical history. It would be more honest to say, "They were wrong; we've discovered new truth in the twentieth century," or "Times have changed, and we must reflect those changes," than to tamper with source material.

In defending the Bible as it stands, I'm not implying that it wouldn't be different in many places if God were revealing Himself today instead of millennia ago. With girl runaways outnumbering boys, the prodigal might well be a daughter, if Jesus were telling His story today. With women's education equal to men's, today's Bible might have books written by holy women. Surely the exploits of women missionaries would be headlined. And Herod might be a woman.

But these changes, reflecting the times with which God was burdened in His self-revelation, would not obscure the original Creation, nor the peculiar identities of men and women. Biblical principles about sex are unchanging.

Thank God for making women different from men.

I think an awful lot of men would agree with me. Men like Abraham and Moses and Aquila and Gloria Steinem's husband, if she's married.

# Why Don't Sinners Cry Anymore?

Not just for cartoons

**October 1974**

About fifteen years ago I wrote some chapters for a book I never finished. One of those chapters was about the lost grace of repentance.

It was occasioned, I think, by British thinker-preacher Martyn Lloyd-Jones's comment that people no longer weep at evangelistic meetings. They laugh, he said, they come happily to the front, but they don't mourn over their sins. Nor does the evangelist indicate that weeping, or repentance, is part of a transaction with God.

It seemed to me then that a lot of Christians felt that repentance was not for this dispensation, that the call of the prophets to repent culminated, and ended, with John the Baptist.

Nothing that has happened in these intervening years has changed my mind. Godly sorrow for sin that leads to repentance (2 Cor. 7:10) is almost totally absent from our preaching and from our lives. The one who enters the kingdom without repentance hardly finds need for it as a resident.

We have lost the ability to say, "I'm sorry," to God and to one another. We have lost it as persons and we have lost it in our churches and we have lost it as a nation. For if Christians do not feel the need to repent, shall we expect non-Christians to do so?

A national leader tells of being invited into former President Nixon's office almost a year before the resignation. The President asked him and others gathered there what they thought he should do about Watergate.

This man, who is a Christian, says that he told the President that the American people are very forgiving. "Even at this date, if you went to them and said, 'I did wrong, I'm sorry. Please forgive me,' they would."

The President listened, then turned to the next person for his suggestion.

I'm inclined to agree with the advice this leader gave the President. I think that up until the very end, almost, an admission of culpability and a plea for forgiveness would have been honored.

According to *New York* magazine, a reporter asked one of the key Watergate participants, "Aren't you and the others sorry for what happened?" His answer: "Contrition is b.s."

I am very aware that tears and sorrow for sin is only part of the truth, that true repentance involves a radical change of conduct. Thus Judas Iscariot "repented" after he betrayed Jesus— the Greek word means he had an "after care," he was sorrowful (Matt. 27:3). But if his mind was not changed, he would not have embarked on a new and different life if his suicide attempt had failed.

The New Testament word for repentance of the kind that pleases God means being sorry enough to change conduct and involves an about-face.

But do we need to repent today? Or is this one of those "works of righteousness" from which God's grace frees us? Jesus taught repentance: "Do you suppose that these Galileans [who died at the hands of Pilate] were sinners above all the Galileans, because they suffered such things? I tell you, No; but unless you repent, you shall all likewise perish" (Luke 13:2, 3).

Peter taught repentance. In his first sermon, on the Day of Pentecost, he said, "Repent and be baptized, every one of you" (Acts 2:38).

Paul taught repentance: "The goodness of God leads you to repentance" (Rom. 2:4). "I have taught you . . . repentance toward God and faith toward our Lord Jesus Christ" (Acts 20:21).

And the last book of the Bible teaches repentance: "Repent, or else I will come to you quickly, and will fight against you with the sword of my mouth" (Rev. 2:16).

Our attitude toward God affects our attitude toward others. Maybe one reason marriage and family relations are in such desperate straits today, including those of Christians, is that we've lost the grace of repentance.

Joseph C. Macaulay, interim pastor of New York's Calvary Baptist Church, told of a visit to the Hebrides Islands some years ago, when revival was going on. On his way to church, where he was to preach, Dr. Macaulay heard a man sobbing in a cottage as he passed.

"What's that?" he asked his companion.

"That's John. He's on his way to God. He'll come through," was the reply.

For many years, the *New Yorker* magazine has had two subjects of cartoons repeated again and again. One is Noah's Ark. The other is of a man with a sandwich sign that reads, "Repent. The end of the world is at hand."

I think we need that message—not just a cartoon, but in our pulpits and in our lives.

# *Power of Providential Praying*

Concerns beyond the family circle

**December 1975**

I'll pray for you."

How often I've said that, only to forget, or to remember for a brief period of time and then forget.

Of course, some people and needs are always present in the mind; there is no need to be reminded to pray for them. Family—immediate and more distant, work and associates, neighbors, pastor and church staff, familiar missionaries and Christian workers, government, the persecuted of earth: these come to mind almost automatically.

A prayer list is a help, perhaps a necessity, for responsible praying. But periodic editing, including both additions and removals, is necessary if it is not to become unwieldy. And often, when time is suddenly available for praying, I find the list is not at hand. (I'll admit that it should probably be always available, but it isn't.) Or I realize I've removed a name for whom I should still be praying.

The result for me, and I suspect for a lot of other people, is recurring guilt over my prayer life—especially intercessory prayer. "When we work, we work; when we pray, God works," is never far from my mind.

In the past couple of years, several things have helped me pray more, and, I trust, pray more effectively.

First is a fresh awareness of God's amazing closeness to me. I am never removed from His presence, except by sin. "Pray without ceasing" (1 Thess. 5:17) means that as I write this on an airplane six miles above western Pennsylvania, I can pause to speak to my Father. Driving a car, sitting at my desk, shaving in the morning are other situations when I can turn to God and find Him there. When I am awakened at night and cannot immediately return to sleep, I can pray to God.

Praying with other people has also been a great encouragement to me: with my wife, when we are alone in the car, with my sons, when I'm driving them to school.

But my greatest help in remembering has come from realizing that God can bring to my mind those people and situations for which I ought to pray. He can stir my memory through associations—something I see, something I hear, something I read. If I forget to pray for someone, He can remind me.

A stewardess on this flight reminds me of a woman whose husband recently died. I pray for that woman and her children. The pilot makes me remember to pray for friends who are also airline pilots, and for JAARS and MAF.*

Driving the car, I see a street name, a billboard advertisement, a real estate sign, a church: each leads to an association that results in prayer.

A friend mentioned something that E. Stanley Jones wrote in connection with prayer; this has been a help to me: If your mind wanders to something else when you're praying, Dr. Jones suggested, pray for that something else.

God can stir our minds to pray: God can bring an image from the past, or from a far distant place, before our mind's eye, and lead us to pray.

Another part of faithfulness in praying for others is not to wait until a convenient, quiet time—rather, to pray in the midst of life's pressures. I think I'm learning this, as well as the rightness of saying, "Let's pray about that now" when someone talks to me about a problem.

We do not pray enough together, as Christian brothers and sisters. We talk, and we forget that our Father is there listening—and that it should be the most natural thing to include Him in our conversation.

Recently I said good-bye to Abe Vander Puy at the Quito, Ecuador airport. As we stood there with people moving past us, Abe said, "Let's pray." His arm went around me, and he committed me, for the trip and for my life to the Lord. It's the most satisfying departure from an airport I've ever had.

"Pray without ceasing" has implications for life that are so daily, too. While driving a car, you see an accident; do you think to pray for the injured one, the worried, upset ones? When you see the poverty-stricken, the old and feeble, the alcoholic on the city streets, do you think to pray for them? God answers prayer; His

---

*Editor's note:* JAARS stands for Jungle Aviation and Radio Service, an arm of Wycliffe Bible Translators, and MAF is Missionary Aviation Fellowship.

answer does not depend on the possibility of our personal intervention in the situation about which we pray.

Prayer may be our children's greatest enlightenment that we have concerns for people and situations beyond our own family circle.

Reading *Time* or *Newsweek* or the daily paper are other occasions to pray. Can God intervene in the Patty Hearst case to bring about justice, to bring about truth? Can God solve the problems of Northern Ireland and Lebanon? Do we ask Him for these things?

I remember one day early in the Watergate affair when I was driving my two sons, one teen-age, the other on the threshold of teen-age, to school. (A year or so earlier, when the federal judge and former Illinois governor Otto Kerner was on trial, one of them said to me, "But doesn't everybody in public office accept bribes? Do any of them live on their salary?" I was suddenly struck with the image he had—and other children probably had—of public servants.) This morning as we prayed together in the car, I asked God to bring truth to light, to make corruption surface, to judge the guilty and protect the innocent.

Later, looking back, I was glad that I had a part—an infinitesimal part, but a part—in the resolution of Watergate, by turning to a judge greater than the Senate or the federal court.

# *Bloodthirsty or Biblical?*

Hang the man or hang the logic

**May 1977**

One element has been missing from discussions of Gary Gilmore's recent execution, and of the larger question of capital punishment.

We've heard a lot, mostly con but some pro, about the deterrent effect of capital punishment, and about the thwarted possibility of reformation. And more has been said about "murder" by the state, about the effect on the condemned man of waiting for time and appeals to run out, about society's voyeurism, even about the suffering of the condemned man compared to that of his victim and the victim's family.

But I have not seen a serious presentation of the one element in capital punishment that has found general historical agreement, among Jews and Christians: retribution, the punitive effect.

Perhaps it's not surprising that this is absent from our consideration of the ultimate punishment, since it is also the missing element from our consideration of punishments for lesser crimes.

I am not especially concerned about the rejection of retribution by the secular mind, which in our day to a large degree is humanistic. Reformation of the criminal is the only reason for incarceration or other punishment, according to this way of thinking. But I am deeply concerned about its rejection by the Christian mind. As in so many other recent instances, it seems to me that we have in this turned from the Word of God and accommodated our theology, attitudes and values to this present evil world and its ruler.

Behind all the Bible's teaching about sin and crime is one central proposition: The reformation of the offender is not the primary object of punishment; nor is the deterrent effect upon others. Rather, punishment is inflicted to satisfy justice. That justice may be God's or (by derivation from God) the state's. Why did God inflict destruction on men at the time of the Flood, in Sodom and Gomorrah and Jerusalem? Not for the good of the offenders or for their reformation, but to satisfy His justice. And God's future punishment of fallen angels and of men who ultimately refuse His offer of salvation likewise will not be for the purpose of reformation; this the Bible rules out by declaring that the punishment is eternal.

The prevention of crime is desired by all who desire justice and righteousness. And this is sometimes a side effect of punishment. But whether capital punishment or lesser punishments are deterrent or not is, for the Bible-believing Christian, irrelevant to the central reason for punishment of the criminal.

Theologian Charles Hodge distinguishes between punishment and chastisement. "A father chastises a child in love, and for the child's good. And God, our heavenly Father, brings suffering upon His children for their edification. But evil inflicted for the benefit of the sufferer is chastisement, and not punishment. Punishment, properly speaking, is evil inflicted in satisfaction of justice."

Punishment of the wicked is always related to the anger of God in the Scriptures. Chastisement of His children is related to love.

Even for God's children, there is punishment as well as discipline. St. Paul relates the sickness and death of many in the Corinthian church to their sin and lack of self-judgment. And we are told that "if we confess our sins, he is faithful and just to forgive us our sins" (1 John 1:9).

Isn't the penalty removed by confession, by saying we're sorry, please forgive us?

No, and here, it seems to me, is the heart of the matter.

The penalty is removed by our Lord Christ's action in taking it upon Himself on the cross. His death was as our substitute. A penalty always results from the violation of law, and that penalty is always borne. It may be borne by the sinner or it may be borne by Christ. It may be borne by the criminal or it may be borne by the victim and by society. But in a moral universe, the penalty is borne; it must be borne.

Retribution is at the heart of our Lord Christ's redemptive work. The sentence imposed by God upon me was death; Christ fulfilled the sentence, bore the punishment, and therefore I am pardoned.

Not all theologians agree with this view. I remember hearing Dr. Clarence T. Craig tell a class in Pauline theology at Union Seminary in New York (commenting on Romans 3, and the concept of propitiation), that any attempt to show that there is something in the essential nature of God that requires the satisfaction of His justice against sinners "ends only in blackening the character of God."

According to an alternative view, it was not necessary for sin to be punished, with judgment falling either on the sinner or on the Son of God. Rather, the death of Christ, along with His life, teaching and other acts, produces a moral effect on the hearts of men. The results of this moral influence (which is what the theory is called) is that the sinner turns from his sin. He is reformed.

I am aware that some Christian theologians hold and have held the moral influence theory of the work of Christ, rather than the substitutionary atonement theory, the punitive theory that I have just mentioned. And it is true that Christ's life and teachings and death exert a powerful influence on the Christian. By His example our Lord does affect our conduct. But this follows the satisfaction of God's just judgment; it does not replace it.

Most theologians have found this theory inadequate. So have most of our Christian organizations and institutions, which incorporate a statement about the substitutionary atonement in their bases of faith.

Now we are back at our initial question: What is the state's purpose in punishing the criminal? Is it simply reformation, or is it the exacting of a penalty, retribution?

According to the Old Testament, homicide is to be punished by the death of the murderer (Ex. 21:12, 14; Lev. 24:17; Num. 24:21; Deut. 19:11, 13). These passages distinguish between murder and manslaughter, providing for escape from the penalty for those guilty only of the latter.

The rationale for capital punishment is found in Genesis 9:6: "Whoever sheds man's blood, by man shall his blood be shed; for in the image of God made he man."

This command was given to Noah, the second head of the human race. Therefore it does not seem to be limited to one particular age or race. Rather, the reason is ageless: Man bears God's image; therefore the destruction of man is an outrage against God, to be punished by execution.

The New Testament confirms the state's authority to carry

out executions in Romans 13:4. And neither Jesus Christ nor St. Paul challenged this authority in their own confrontations with the state. In fact, St. Paul affirmed it: "If I be an offender, or have committed anything worthy of death, I refuse not to die" (Acts 25:11).

As Christian people, we believe that there are unavoidable results of disobeying God, whether the disobedience is personal or national. If this is so, whether capital punishment is a deterrent to murder or not, we are suffering those results as a nation and will suffer them in the future.

Again quoting Hodge: "Experience teaches that where human life is undervalued, it is insecure; that where the murderer escapes with impunity or is inadequately punished, homicides are fearfully multiplied. The practical question, therefore, is "Who is to die? The innocent man or the murderer?"

The Old Testament prophets ("All Scripture is given by inspiration of God and is profitable" [2 Tim. 3:16]) pronounced God's judgment on nations, including Israel, and cities that were characterized by violence and the shedding of innocent blood. The judgments they mentioned are frightening, as were their later fulfillment.

And is God not already visiting judgment on our callous disregard of human life, as children murder parents; parents murder children, including infants; teens and young adults kill old people; arsonists kill ghetto-dwellers, lust-ridden men rape and kill innocent women; bombers and sharpshooters kill numbers of innocent people?

I am aware that some who read what I have written will ascribe bloodthirstiness to me, desire for vengeance, lack of Christian concern for a brother human being who happened to commit murder.

I am also aware that when it was still practiced by the state, capital punishment fell most heavily on the poor and members of minority races. The rich, who could afford prestigious lawyers, often went free. God punishes nations for unequal treatment of the guilty. God's people must crusade for justice in all areas, including capital crimes.

I am thankful for decisions of the Supreme Court in recent years that have reinforced equal treatment under the law, for instance requiring legal counsel for the poor and indigent.

And if the viewpoint I espoused is considered bloodthirsty, what shall we say of a nation that gets its "kicks" out of watching murders and other acts of violence as a chief form of entertainment—in television, movies, theater? A nation that is made up of increasing numbers of onlookers who watch other human beings beaten, raped, and murdered in real life, without intervening? A nation that seriously discusses televising (with sponsor) the execution of murderers?

We're sick.

God, heal us. Soon.

# The Me Generation

## What a small package

### October 1977

Tom Wolfe, the innovative journalist, has called this present era the "Me Generation."

We are obsessed with ourselves, our bodies, our gratification, our pleasure. We judge every situation by its effect on us.

Writing in the *Yale Review,* Dr. Fred Bloom, a psychiatrist, tells about one woman, a social worker, who divorced her husband because he wasn't helping her grow as a person, "A therapeutic conception of marriage that would have surprised Freud."

If my wife does not help me grow, I dissolve our marriage. If I think I would find greater pleasure, perhaps the fountain of youth, in young flesh, I dissolve our marriage. If my wife has fallen behind me in intellectual growth and ability to relate to the business and social groups I aspire to—regardless of the fact that her faithfulness in providing a home and raising our children caused the gap—I dissolve our marriage.

Or an extreme example: I heard of a man whose wife was diagnosed as having cancer. His first reaction? "I'll divorce her."

The Me Generation.

I wish this only described the ordinary secular person, the one with no resource in God, the one without hope for the future, without any knowledge that present sufferings are to be endured—suffered—rather than shed, because they are for only a moment, while they lead to a "far more exceeding and eternal weight of glory" (2 Cor. 4:17).

Sadly, the Me Generation description also fits many Christians, who are "blinded by the god of this world" (2 Cor. 4:4). Call the god Satan or flesh or pride or me, it matters little.

I think we who struggle for maturity take comfort in the wrong places. We read Gail Sheehy's *Passages* and say, "That's me. That's where I'm at," instead of recognizing that the patterns she describes are of secular, not Christian, man/woman. They may describe our experience, but they do not authenticate it as other than human (without the operation of divine grace), or make certain parts of it right from a moral standpoint.

Some years ago, I heard the late William Culbertson, then president of Moody Bible Institute, speak on the "dangers of the middle mile." With great seriousness and emphasis he said, "I fear lest I should not end well."

"What an awful thing to say," was the response of a Christian woman, after I had later repeated Dr. Culbertson's words in a meeting where I was speaking. "Why it sounds as if he has no faith in God."

No, it's not lack of faith in God that makes a man say that; it's lack of faith in himself. And that lack of faith may be related to the experiences of other Christians he has observed over a lifetime.

Or it may even arise out of reading the Bible. The mid-life crisis is not some new discovery by our super-brilliant American psychologists. Saul went through it. So did David. And Solomon. They make good case studies—at least as good as the ones Sheehy documents.

Years ago, a Christian leader who was married and in middle age had an affair with another woman. His wife became aware of the infatuation, saw it grow into something serious and destructive. (I know little about their previous relationship; it may not have been too good.) Then the board of his church became aware of it and dismissed him. Belatedly, he returned to his wife, breaking the other relationship. In those days, it wasn't so easy to find another church after this sort of severance, so he found a position in business.

One Sunday, at Sunday school time, this couple entered another church which they had not visited previously. A man at the door asked if they needed help in finding where they should go, since there were several classes for adults. Which one did they want?

"I guess I belong in the nursery department," the former pastor replied.

Few insights could be more honest or revealing. I respected the man for understanding this and admitting it. Those words had the ring of David's response in Psalm 51.

But to avoid the trap, rather than to be released from it, severely injured: what Christian person, young or old, wouldn't give anything to keep from ending up in the nursery department?

Perhaps we should give a man and a woman two choices in their marriage vows: either "I take you for better or for worse," or "only for better"; "for richer or for poorer," or "only for richer"; "in sickness and in health," or "as long as you stay well and attractive"; "till death us do part," or "till I find someone who pleases me more."

At least people wouldn't be breaking their promise to God and to their partner later, when they opt for youth or scintillating conversation or no responsibility for children or what they perceive to be upward mobility—which may turn into downward mobility to a hell of guilt.

I don't want to give the impression by what I write here that Christians are the only ones who honor their vows. Thank God there still is a deep pure spring of faithfulness in marriage flowing in American life. I knew one man whose wife was totally incapacitated by a stroke. For nine years, until he himself was struck down, he took care of her total needs. After that long period, she had no bedsores. Two weeks after she was put in a nursing home, she developed them; another two weeks and she died.

Our whole family spoke of Christ's saving grace to that magnificent old man. He listened, but without outward response. I hope he responded before he died; surely the Spirit must push such a man in life's closing moments.

I think of that man when I hear a seemingly mature Christian man or woman rationalize their desertion (ugly, accurate word) of spouse and children.

And so often I think of Thomas à Kempis's words, centuries ago: "When you see a brother stumble and fall, your first thought should be, I am most likely to fall in the same way." God keep me from it.

Me. What a small package. And it gets smaller and smaller apart from Christ in me and obedience to His will.

# Bobby Kennedy's Thanksgiving

Two Brazilian missionaries serve an unexpected guest

**November 1978**

It was the last Thursday of November 1967, the day their friends from the United States called Thanksgiving. Desmond and Grace Derbyshire were not planning to celebrate; they were British. So that particular Thursday would pass like all the other days at their remote jungle outpost in northern Brazil. Or so they thought.

Des and Grace were missionaries associated with Wycliffe Bible Translators, working from sunup to sundown on a translation of the Bible into the language of the Hixkaryana Indians, a primitive tribe.

The morning was hot, and Grace was having a bath. Her tub, a hollowed-out log—actually a canoe that had not been shaped on the outside—was a gift from her husband.

Suddenly Grace looked up at the sky. Surely that was the sound of an approaching plane. But the JAARS (Jungle Aviation and Radio Service, an arm of Wycliffe) plane wouldn't be coming with mail and supplies for weeks. And this plane had a more powerful engine. Who could it be?

She heard the plane circle, then come down on the river and taxi to shore. A few minutes later Des came running up to the place where her bathtub was concealed by a heavy growth of tropical foliage.

"Hurry and get dressed," he said. "We have guests: Bobby Kennedy and his party are here from the United States."

"Bobby Kennedy? The brother of John?"

"Yes. He's just finishing a tour of South America, ending up here in Brazil. He expressed a desire to visit an Indian tribe before he returns home, and the government suggested ours."

"Isn't today an American holiday?"

"Yes it is, Thanksgiving."

"We'll have to provide some sort of special meal. How many of them are there?"

"Six or seven."

Grace groaned. "Our food supply is nil."

"You'll find something," Des said in that lighthearted manner of husbands who know their wives' genius at innovating.

And Grace did. It wasn't turkey, or roast beef with Yorkshire pudding; it was chicken, provided by the Indians—almost as if history were repeating itself three centuries later. Fried bananas were a good substitute for cranberry sauce.

After the feast, all the men went to a sandy beach on the river and skinny-dipped. There was a lot of light banter; Kennedy's group reflected the easy-going relationship that resulted from several weeks traveling together.

"Hey," one of them said as Bobby Kennedy (then Senator from New York) stood waist deep in water, "this would be a great time for you to announce that you'll be a candidate for the Presidency. We could photograph you making the announcement."

Everyone laughed.

In the evening, after the sun had gone down, the little group sat around the screened area of the small house. A group of Indians joined them.

Robert Kennedy asked the Indians questions which Des translated into the Hixkaryana language. He then translated their replies into English.

Des and Grace will never forget one particular question.

"Ask him," Kennedy said, pointing at one of the Hixkaryanas, "what he'd do if he had a couple of hours free. That is, what does he like to do more than anything else?"

Whether by coincidence or by divine plan, the Indian he indicated was one who had trusted Jesus, an early and continuing trophy of God's grace among the Hixkaryanas.

Des translated the question. After a moment the Indian spoke; his reply was brief.

"He says he'd read the Bible," Des translated. "They don't have the whole Bible yet—Grace and I will be translating for some years to come just to finish the New Testament."

Robert Kennedy turned toward the entourage and repeated, "He'd read the Bible. He wouldn't choose to hunt or fish; he'd want to read the Bible."

Soon after goodnights were said, sleeping bags were brought out, and Thanksgiving Day 1967 was over.

The next morning Des and Grace waved as the plane took off, then returned to the routine of translating.

Seven months later, his candidacy announced, Robert Kennedy was assassinated in a Los Angeles hotel.

About a year ago the Derbyshires finished their translation of the New Testament, and the printed volume was dedicated to the Hixkaryana tribe.

# Sorting Sin's Laundry
**May 1979**

People in general, Christian people in particular, tend to divide sins into two categories: their sins and our sins.

The Bible, of course, knows no such distinction. Sin is sin, without partiality shown to the sins of God's people—our sins.

Drunkenness is their sin, so we preach against drinking. Covetousness is our sin, so we seldom mention it, even though it is given equal billing with drunkenness in 1 Corinthians 6:10.

I was talking with my daughter, who has taught in public schools, about the undesirability of having homosexuals as teachers.

Her reply: "The bigger problem I've seen isn't homosexuals, but heterosexual men who can't keep their hands off the girls they teach."

Nobody is leading a crusade against men who molest girls or seduce their students. Yet there is such a crusade against homosexuals.

Why?

I think it's because homosexual sins are their sins, heterosexual sins are ours.

The same Bible that says, "Thou shalt not commit homosexual acts" (1 Cor. 6:9) also says "Thou shalt not commit adultery" (Ex. 20:14). Yet most evangelical churches are very uptight about homosexuality, relatively very accepting of adultery and the concomitant problems of desertion and divorce.

In fact, if there is one sin that could destroy the church's witness it isn't homosexuality; it's disobedience of God's commands in the area of heterosexual marriage.

We're all familiar with the passage that teaches how God gave men of a reprobate mind up to homosexual acts (Rom. 1:27). We've heard those verses quoted a lot in the past couple of years. Denominations are in danger of being split over the problem.

Can you name another sin that God says he gave men up to, in that same passage? Yes, murder. Yes, hatred of God. Yes, the invention of evil things.

You didn't mention gossip (Rom. 1:29).

Why? I think it's because those other things are their sins, gossip is ours. So we never preach on it or write about it.

Lest I be misunderstood, let me say that the increasing acceptance of a homosexual lifestyle—like our acceptance of violence—seems to me to be a sign of accelerating decline of our civilization and that salt's savor.

Yet it's possible that more children have been lost to the church as a result of gossip and backbiting than as a result of homosexual seduction.

# *"Where Do You Get Ideas?"*

## Column writing involves "housecleaning"

## October 1979

"**A**mericans will not accept suffering as part of the natural order of things. This exasperates any European. Americans still cling to the absurd idea that it ought to be possible to be happy. . . . The great difference between America and the Old World, by and large, is that parents in the Old World expect their children to do no better than themselves, while parents in

America, by and large, expect, and justifiably, their children to do better. And it is not far-fetched to see a reflection of this attitude in the wondrous way in which the inconvenience of even a small snowfall is regarded as having the proportions of a disaster. There should be no snow, except on holidays. There should be no poverty, except for those who choose it" (Henry Fairlie, *Manchester Guardian*).

\* \* \*

The test of Christian repentance for sin is recognition that God was hurt, not man. In David's words: "Against thee, thee only, have I sinned, and done this evil in thy sight" (Ps. 51:4).

\* \* \*

In Genesis 2:9, "Out of the ground the Lord God made to grow every tree that is *pleasant to the sight* and good for food." God is interested in beauty as well as nutrition.

\* \* \*

"Last Sunday I saw my elderly uncle. He said, 'It won't be long now.' He has always been proud of his gardening skills and said, 'When I get up there, I'm sure going to show them how to grow onions.' I asked him if he was afraid to die (so much Scripture seems to say, 'Be not afraid'). His reply with a still, husky voice was, 'If I were freezing would I be afraid of a warm breeze?'" (from a friend).

# Swift to Forgive

Cheap grace in the Me generation

## November 1979

The *New Yorker* recently carried a semi-serious piece titled "Attitude," by Garrison Keillor, about how to play slow-pitch softball, "a game that lets me go through the motions of baseball without getting beaned or having to run too hard." Keillor's approach to the game is casual: "If a player's wife or girlfriend wants to play, we give her a glove and send her out to right field, no questions asked."

The writer describes two incidents.

"Bottom of the ninth, down 18–3, two outs, a man on first and a woman on third, and our third baseman strikes out. Strikes out! In slow-pitch, not even your grandmother strikes out, but this guy does, and after his third strike—a wild swing at a ball that bounces on the plate—he topples over in the dirt and lies flat on his back, laughing. *Laughing!*

"Same game, earlier. They have the bases loaded. A weak grounder is hit toward our second baseperson. The runners are running. She picks up the ball, and she looks at them. She looks at first, at second, at home. We yell, 'Throw it! Throw it!' and she throws it, underhand at the pitcher, who has turned and run to back up the catcher. The ball rolls across the third-base line and under the bench. Three runs score. The batter, a fatso, chugs into second. The other team hoots and hollers, and what does she do? She shrugs and smiles ('Oh, silly me'); after all, it's only a game. Like the aforementioned strikeout artist, she treats her error as a joke."

Then comes Keillor's insightful comment: "They have forgiven themselves instantly, which is unforgivable. It is we who should forgive them, who can say, 'It's all right, it's only a game.' They are supposed to throw up their hands and kick the dirt and hang their heads, as if this boner, even if it is their sixteenth of the afternoon—this is the one that really and truly breaks their hearts.

"That attitude sweetens the game for everyone. The sinner feels sweet remorse. The fatso feels some sense of accomplishment; this is no bunch of rum-dums he forced into an error but a team with some class. We, the sinner's teammates, feel momentary anger at her—dumb! dumb play!—but then, seeing her grief, we sympathize with her in our hearts (any one of us might have made that mistake or one worse), and we yell encouragement, including the shortstop, who, moments before, dropped an easy throw for a force at second. 'That's all right! Come on! We got 'em! we yell. Shake it off! These turkeys can't hit!'

"They have forgiven themselves instantly, which is unforgivable. It is we who should forgive them."

Beyond slow-pitch softball, way beyond, the problem of self-forgiveness without the forgiveness of others exists today.

Many years ago an evangelist was scheduled to hold meetings in a small Minnesota town. The laypeople who were planning the meetings learned of his involvement in a long-standing adulterous relationship with his secretary. When one of them visited the evangelist and confronted him with the allegation, his response was, "Yes, it's true; I'll admit it to my wife; let's get on with the meetings." He instantly forgave himself; he saw no need for forgiveness from others.

Those laypeople canceled the meetings.

Another day, another field, another play. The wife of a Christian leader discovers a pattern of her husband's infidelity that extends back several years. He admits the truth, then says, "Let's just start afresh."

She initiates proceedings for a divorce, to his surprise and hurt. He forgave himself; why couldn't she forgive him?

A Christian statesman tells of being summoned to the Oval Office, along with a group of other leaders, by then-President Richard M. Nixon a few months before his resignation, but after the famous tapes had been made public.

"What do you think I should do?" the President asked.

When his turn to answer came, the Christian answered, "Mr. President, the American people are a very forgiving people. Even now, if you went on TV and confessed the wrongs you and your associates have done, and asked to be forgiven, it is my opinion that they would forgive you and give you another chance."

The President said, "Next."

Mr. Nixon forgave himself; he did not seem to have felt the need for forgiveness from his associates and his country.

And the Lord's Prayer: It doesn't say, "Help us forgive ourselves," but "Forgive us our debts as we forgive our debtors" (Matt. 6:12)—and seek forgiveness from those to whom we are indebted, starting with the Chief Creditor.*

---

*\*Editor's note:* In response to this article Dad received the following letter dated December 12, 1979:

Dear Mr. Bayly:

    It was a wonderful surprise to see my name in your column since I used to enjoy your stuff when you wrote for *His* magazine. (Maybe you still write for them, but I don't read it anymore.) I seem to recall that you wrote a comic novel about an evangelist who traveled around in a balloon. I tried to find it once—now I'll try again.

    As for your quoting from the softball piece, that's fine, but don't forget that the complete player is not only hard on himself but also hard on umpires. On close calls that go against him, he looks at the ump as if the ump has grown a second head. The runner is safe? *Safe?* You mean, like *not out?* He shakes his head, tosses the ball to the pitcher, and trudges back to his position. He mumbles. I see too little of that from church teams. They're too compliant.

    Best Wishes,
    Garrison Keillor

# PART THREE

# OUT OF MY MIND: THE EIGHTIES

# JOSEPH T. BAYLY:
# IN APPRECIATION
*by Kent Hughes*

When I first met Joe Bayly it was late in his life and early in my ministry—some thirteen years ago when I was called to pastor College Church, Joe's church for over twenty years.

My first glimpse of Joe was as he sat Quaker-bearded with his wife Mary Lou on the front pew listening benignly (like the face on the oatmeal box) to my forgettable candidating sermon. How would I fare, I wondered, with this smiling but nevertheless imposing personality, the author of the sometimes acerbic *Eternity* magazine column "Out of My Mind?"

Happily, I learned the smile was real and that Joe Bayly cared little about where I came from and still less about my pedigree. Indeed, among the first things he said to me was in reference to the church's highly educated congregation—"Just remember, Pastor, we all slip our trousers on one leg at a time." Joe was put off by anyone and anything that smacked of condescension, especially smarmy preachers and academic canard. He was, in fact, a spiritual populist because he truly believed that he could learn from everyone—and thus treated all his acquaintances with equal respect.

As it turned out, Barbara and I became close friends of Joe and Mary Lou, so that in addition to our occasional meals together, our family was regularly included as part of the Bayly family gatherings during the holidays and such memorable events as sipping apple cider while Joe sat in his rocking chair and read out loud Truman Capote's haunting *Christmas Memory.*

But what most stands out about the Bayly get-togethers was the conversation between Joe and his then grown children and anyone else at table. Joe had brought his children up to reason biblically and logically about everything—so conversation was always laced with spirited, cheerful, family forthrightness and iconoclasm. If you had the temerity to state your viewpoint you had better be ready to defend it—"You believe that?" No quarter was extended—especially to Joe himself. Joe was profoundly biblical in his thinking which meant, for example, on social issues he would sometimes come down on the so-called "liberal" side of a question, and other times the decidedly "conservative" side. This could be unsettling to anyone with a tendency to doctrinaire or conventional expression. And of course, this is one of the reasons why Joe was something of a gadfly to the evangelical enterprise. No bromides, trendy or conventional, ever fell from Joe Bayly's pen because he was rigorously orthodox and biblical, and therefore gloriously radical!

Joe Bayly was, in a word, a prophet—and to us a voice of sanity in an upside-down world. His writings were always penetrating whether humoring us to greater idealism and faith as he did in *I Saw Gooley Fly,* or steeling us for the future with the Orwellian chill of *Winterflight.* Joe was a straight shooter and fighter—where principle was involved. And this left him with his share of enemies. But agree or disagree, like him or not, he was never equivocating or disingenuous. His trademark clarity and economy of expression left no doubt about where he stood.

He personally made us feel safe. Midst the confusion, there was always Joe Bayly, who rejected weak-minded reasoning and thought things through, kindly telling us what he thought, right or wrong. Joe made us stand up for what we believed.

Those who personally knew him knew that his prophetic ministry was practically toned by his rich familial relationships, his capacity for friendship, and his commitment to the Church. Mary Lou, his "wife of forty two winters" to use Joe's expression, and his four surviving children all reflect this and, indeed, enriched his gift for relating truth to life.

As his pastor and friend, I witnessed firsthand his belief in the Church. For years, he team-taught the "Covenant Class," a transgenerational Sunday school class of grandparents, parents, their college-age children, and singles including unmarried, divorced, and widowed. The Bayly home regularly hosted numerous singles. Though super busy, Joe also served as an Elder-prophet-writer-poet-preacher-business executive. In this regard it is highly significant that his children are all busy in ministry.

Deborah, the oldest, is the principal of Lake View Academy, which ministers in reclaiming students who have dropped out of the Chicago school system. His three sons Timothy, David, and Nathan are all pastors.

Joe Bayly always brought with him a sense of the numinous—that life is supernatural and that there is always *plus ultra*—more beyond. To be sure this had much to do with the early death of three of his children. But it was also due to his radically biblical mind-set—he determined to set his mind on things above. In fact, I heard him say it in his final sermon at College Church—"Oh God, burn eternity into my eyeballs. Help me to see all of this life through the perspective of eternity." God used Joe Bayly to do this for thousands of us.

Perhaps once a month I say to my wife, "I miss Joe Bayly," and we smile and agree that no one has come to replace him—at least for us.

> —Kent Hughes, Pastor
> College Church in Wheaton (Illinois)
> October 26, 1992

# Empty Calories

**February 1980**

George Kraft is a retired member of Overseas Missionary Fellowship (OMF), a veteran worker with China Inland Mission. Detained by the communists in 1950, Mr. Kraft continued his ministry (with Mrs. Kraft) in Taiwan and Singapore.

Mr. Kraft interrupted a silence of many years by writing to me several months ago in response to one of these columns. His letter is disturbing to me; it is also beautiful in its expression of the deepening of a husband/wife relationship through suffering. With his permission, I share the following excerpts:

> More than forty years of marriage plus [his wife's] terminal cancer bring new joy and meaning to our marriage vow, "till death do us part." But almost weekly we are pained with news of the marriage breakup of evangelical leaders so that one almost wants to cry out, "Stop! For God's sake stop!" What's happening, Joe?
>
> ... Many years ago I read an article by a German Lutheran theologian with which I strongly disagreed at the time. But now I wonder if he did not have some legitimate insights. As I recall in his thesis he maintained that the pietistic emphasis was dangerous and in some cases bordered on heresy and that its fruits would be bitter. As I considered the Moravian missionary movement, some of the rich devotional hymns coming from the pietistic sources and the obvious devotion to the person of Christ I dismissed his work as more of the dead orthodoxy against which I had rebelled in my youth. But there was more to his thesis than mere protest. He maintained that the solid theology of the church fathers with its emphasis on Christ and objective truth rather than on subjective experience was much more productive of true scriptural holiness than pietism.

> For some decades now American evangelicals have been feeding upon pietistic literature. . . . I have enjoyed reading them myself but along with my wife have often had a gnawing feeling that something was amiss in the emphasis. What has been the fruitage from this type of thinking? Has it produced vigorous, loyal, covenant-keeping, vow-respecting believers? Or has it induced a sloppy sort of sentimentality which passes for the real thing in undiscerning circles? Has this type of mindset contributed to or at least failed to prevent the marital problems which have produced so much heartache in evangelical circles? This needs to be explored by someone who can put things in perspective. No names and books need be mentioned but the deeper issues do need to be brought forth. For as a man or a generation thinks in their hearts so are they (Prov. 23:7). And sloppy, sentimental thinking will not produce strong homes for God and his church.

Pearl Kraft, George's wife, recently died, after what was described as "an incredible illness" of almost seven years, that involved much suffering and constant care. A memorial fund has been established by OMF, and will be used for scholarships at Singapore Bible College, and an OMF-sponsored gospel broadcast to China.

I'm inclined to comment on the beauty of a long marriage in the Lord, which inevitably involves some suffering, and to say that Christian growth and the development of a personality are rooted in such a relationship—not in the "I need space in which to grow, I'll divorce you for my own good" type of thinking that is so prevalent in the world, and even in the church, today.

But the essential point of George Kraft's letter goes far beyond the crisis in marriage. It extends to Christian morality and ethics in every area of life, in every business and profession, to priorities established by the Church, to our parachurch organizations and institutions.

We need a rebirth of Christian doctrine, of biblical theology. We need iron in place of straw, emphasis on God's work through suffering in place of this overweening emphasis on success and growth.

Maybe a good goal for the decade just beginning would be one doctrinal sermon every month. We've had enough milk; bring on the meat (Heb. 5:12).

# New Fig-Leaf Dictionary
## May 1980

Language changes. Today's understandable words will be tomorrow's quaint archaisms. And yesterday's clear expressions seem old-fashioned and outmoded today.

As an example, it is probable that a majority of people in the United States, for that matter the world, would consider the statement "As American as McDonalds" clear, and the statement "As American as apple pie" obsolete—an archaism.

The church is no exception. Yesterday's words and the ideas they represent pass out of vogue, become archaic; they are replaced with new and different concepts.

Here are some archaisms of biblical and theological derivation, familiar to past generations of Christians, words that seem to have been discarded or replaced by new words and the ideas they represent.

*Adultery:* "Voluntary sexual intercourse between a married man and someone other than his wife, or between a married woman and someone other than her husband" (*Webster's New Collegiate Dictionary,* 1975 ed.). Biblical usage: "Thou shalt not commit adultery" (Ex. 20:14).

"Affair" is the less judgmental word used today. The concept itself is not generally mentioned in preaching, even when divorce is discussed.

*Awe:* "Emotion in which dread, veneration, and wonder are

variously mingled, as: (a) A profound and humbly fearful reverence inspired by deity or by something sacred or mysterious; (b) submissive and admiring fear inspired by authority or power; (c) wondering reverence tinged with fear inspired by the sublime" (*Webster's*). Biblical usage: "Let all the earth fear the Lord: let all the inhabitants of the world stand in awe of him" (Ps. 33:8).

Awe was damaged in the churches, destroyed by the electronic church. Awe has been replaced by good feelings toward oneself and God, by a happy-face image of God.

*Cleave:* "To adhere firmly and closely and loyally and unwaveringly, syn. stick" (*Webster's*). Biblical usage: "For this cause shall a man leave father and mother, and shall cleave to his wife. And they two shall be one flesh" (Matt. 19:5).

"Loyally," "unwaveringly," "stick," "one flesh" are related archaic terms. "Cleave" is only used in its other sense: "Divide, split, separate into distinct parts."

*Guilt:* "The fact of having committed a breach of conduct, especially violating law and involving a penalty" (*Webster's*). Biblical usage: "When one has sinned and become guilty, he shall restore what he took by robbery, or what he got by oppression, or the deposit which was committed to him, or the lost thing which he found, or anything about which he has sworn falsely; he shall restore it in full, and shall add a fifth to it, and give it to him to whom it belongs, on the day of his guilt offering" (Lev. 6:4, 5 RSV).

"Feeling guilty" in current usage has replaced guilt, which is archaic. Feeling guilty is bad; it may lead to deeper emotional problems.

*Hate:* "To feel extreme enmity toward" (*Webster's*). Biblical usage: "Hate evil and love good, and establish justice in the gate . . . I hate, I despise your feasts, and I take no delight in your solemn assemblies. . . . Take away from me the noise of your songs; to the melody of your harps I will not listen. But let justice roll down like waters, and righteousness like an everflowing stream" (Amos 5:15, 21, 23–24 RSV).

Today hatred is perceived to be a harmful, destructive emotion for human beings (including Christians), and is antithetical to an image of the God of love.

*Humble:* "Not proud or haughty; not arrogant or assertive" (*Webster's*). Biblical usage: "If my people, which are called by my name, shall humble themselves, and pray, and seek my face, and turn from their wicked ways; then will I hear from heaven, and will forgive their sin, and will heal their land" (2 Chron. 7:14). During World War II this verse was frequently quoted in Christian assemblies. Numerous days of prayer and prayer meetings were held on the basis of this divine promise.

Today the word is archaic; no national crisis has caused Christians generally to act upon it. This may be related to a rightful feeling of strength among Christians, based upon George Gallup Jr.'s research. "Growing," "successful," "respectable" are now used instead of humble.

*Pollute:* "To make . . . morally impure; defile" (*Webster's*). Biblical usage: "For if after they have escaped the pollutions of the world through the knowledge of the Lord and Savior Jesus Christ, they are again entangled therein, and overcome, the latter end is worse with them than the beginning" (2 Peter 2:20). In the 1930s movies were considered a polluting influence by many boycotting Christians.

Today this idea is considered quaint, narrow, archaic. There is a great resistance to the concept of TV as a moral and spiritual pollutant in the living room. Any use of the term is limited to *Webster's* secondary definition: "To contaminate (an environment) especially with man-made waste." Theological status is given the idea of polluting air, land, oceans, etc. today.

*Repent:* "To be sorry. To turn from sin and dedicate oneself to the amendment of one's life" (*Webster's*). Biblical usage: "The men of Nineveh shall rise in judgment with this generation, and shall condemn it: because they repented at the preaching of Jonah; and behold, a greater than Jonah is here" (Matt. 12:41).

Individual repentance is a lost emphasis in most preaching and evangelism today, as evidenced by the lack of sorrow (tears). When repentance is used, it is applied to social injustice, the rape of the environment, United States intervention in Vietnam, etc.

*Sunday:* "The first day of the week: the Christian analogue of the Jewish Sabbath" (*Webster's*). Biblical usage: "If you turn back your foot from the sabbath, from doing your pleasure on my holy day, and call the sabbath a delight and the holy day of the Lord honorable; if you honor it, not going your own ways, or seeking your own pleasure, or talking idly; then you shall take delight in the Lord, and I will make you ride upon the heights of the earth; I will feed you with the heritage of Jacob your father, for the mouth of the Lord has spoken" (Isa. 58:13–14 RSV). Earlier in this century, when American Christians worked six days a week, eight to ten hours each day, they set apart one day—Sunday—for God.

Today the Christian Sabbath (or Lord's Day) is an archaic concept, probably because there are too many things to do to set one day apart for God and deeds of mercy.

*Vow:* "A solemn promise or assertion; specifically by which a person binds himself to an act, service, or condition" (*Webster's*). Biblical usage: "When you make a vow to the Lord your God, you shall not be slack to pay it; for the Lord your God will surely require it of you, and it would be sin in you. But if you refrain from vowing, it shall be no sin in you. You shall be careful to perform what has passed your lips, for you have voluntarily vowed to the Lord your God what you have promised with your mouth" (Deut. 23:21–23 RSV). The word has been used in a church context of the promises made in the wedding ceremony, before God and to the other person, to cleave to the spouse "for better or for worse, for richer or for poorer, in sickness and in health, until death us do part."

—This is only a beginning. To be really impressed with Christian archaisms, read a theology text written before 1940. Better still, read the Bible.

# One Sage's Testament

## July/August 1980

*It was the summer of 1940. The Netherlands had fallen. A surgeon, talking to an elderly Friesian farmer, asked, "And what are we to do now?" The old Christian replied, "Before men we must be as eagles; before God, as worms."*

Last week, on my sixtieth birthday, I had a warning of my mortality, that a day is coming when my voice in this world will be stilled and I shall awaken in my Lord's awesome, joyous presence.

The warning was a tap on the shoulder, not hands around my neck or a shove to the ground. But it caused me to think deep thoughts, consider separations, ponder my life and work.

I found peace, "the peace of God that surpasses understanding" (Phil. 4:7). Not anxiety, not fear, but peace: the peace of those who know that no force, not even death itself, can come between us and the love of Christ (Rom. 8:35–39).

"The just [those who have been justified before God through faith in his Son] shall live by faith" (Rom. 1:17; Gal. 3:11). Yes, but the just shall die by faith also.

One heavy thought that came to me was what final testament I would leave for my children, our own and other Christians of their generation. This was not a new thought; in recent weeks—perhaps in anticipation of my birthday—it had been recurrent. But now there was an edge of urgency to it: I could not avoid the evidence that my generation is in the process of turning the game over to a fresh team.

Here are some parts of that testament.

1. Read the Bible. Read it all and read it carefully. Read it first and last with your own eyes, but in between read it with the eyes of the poor, the persecuted, the dispossessed, the uneducat-

ed, the prisoner, the stranger, the minority person. By that I mean consciously acknowledge that this isn't just a private pillow of precious promises (a sign of my age: I've avoided alliteration previously), but the voice of the Judge of the Universe.

There are two dangers in reading the Bible. The first is private interpretation, which means coming up with ideas and dogmas that are "original" with you. Check your interpretations with those of other Christians, both writers and speakers who have the gift of understanding God's Word and teaching it.

The second danger is not so obvious, but is at least as serious: Watch out that you don't accept the private interpretations of anyone else. As I see it, this is a grave danger today. Test the ideas and interpretations of Christian leaders, preachers, seminar leaders, and gurus by the Bible. That includes any ideas you've learned from me.

I know this isn't new to you, but I'm amazed at how many Christians follow teachers who start with a statement and then find proof texts to support it. More often than not the texts must be warped ever so slightly or isolated from the context to "prove" the idea.

Don't let anyone trade on your respect for God's Word by winning you to his/her private interpretation of it. And remember that heresies have seldom arisen full-blown; they were first of all the seeds of warped ideas from seemingly godly leaders.

2. There is one "simple" idea in the Christian faith. That is salvation by faith alone in Jesus Christ. Never complicate that wondrous provision of God. When I was a teenager, my confidence in God's power was immeasurably strengthened life-long by seeing hopeless alcoholics in New York missions saved from their derelict ways, reunited with their families, and living for God; all this by merely responding with faith to that simple message and the Spirit's invitation.

Now this may be a slight overstatement, but after we enter God's family by faith, I believe there are only a few uncomplicated ideas or courses of Christian action. Choices must be made, sometimes, in a murky mist, and paradoxes resolved—or lived with. Things don't always turn out right on this tent-ground. So watch out for Christian leaders who would seek to entice you with their simplistic, foolproof, guaranteed answers. It's appealing to a sincere Christian when an obviously authoritative person says, "This is the way and here are the verses to prove it" (note *verses,* not usually *chapters* or *sections*). Be discerning as you listen to that person; don't entrust him/her with your inner soul. And be careful with other people who quote him/her as final authority.

(I have yet to hear a poor or persecuted Christian give a seminar on success as the result of learning biblical principles. And I have yet to hear a hurting Christian parent lecture on the foolproof biblical way to raise teenagers.)

3. Look for humility in the leaders you choose to follow, the voices you choose to hear. Pride, I increasingly believe, is the most damnable sin: the creature's refusal to acknowledge that he/she is a creature responsible to the Creator. No person can foster the impression that he/she is great and then exalt a great God.

A true leader for God speaks and acts with authority. This may (and should) be coupled with humility and meekness. But their aim is to build disciples for Jesus Christ, not their own personal disciples. He/she is horrified to hear people quote them as the authority for their beliefs or actions.

Look for God's little heroes. Let others adulate the Christian superstars. And when you find them encourage them, appreciate them, love them.

4. If God should lead you into a ministry of counseling others, be careful lest you take the place of God in their lives. Never back people—including your children—into a corner where freedom of decision is destroyed. Never manipulate people. And if a person responds to the Holy Spirit's urgings through you, cut the umbilical cord as quickly as possible. Don't get your kicks out of a person's continuing spiritual dependency on you.

I hear a lot of talk about "discipling" today. I'm disturbed by much of it (and much "shepherding"). We must want to make people disciples of Jesus Christ, not of ourselves. One of God's most beautiful gifts is freedom; don't let anyone prevent you from exercising it by coming between you and God. And don't let any group, either.

5. You won't be able to stem the national tide that is running against the family. But determine that your marriage, if God gives you a partner, will be inviolable, that it will continue until death separates for a time. Make your home an oasis of morality and love in a pagan world.

6. Train your children for persecution. I hope it won't come, but prepare them for it. Work toward building a tough character that will stand in the evil day. Read the Bible to your children and pray with them daily. And do other activities with them: take walks, play games, read books aloud. Where will the time come from? Don't have TV. Refuse to rent your living room and your time—your own, your spouse's, your children's—to pagan hucksters. Ask whether you'd want these people as guests and friends in your home, if you'd want your children to grow up under their influence. And ask similar questions about Christian hucksters. Is their image of God, the Christian life, the Church, the biblical one you want "sold" to your children?

Perhaps persecution won't come in your children's lifetime, but the same principles will prepare them for an increasingly popularized evangelical Christianity or a period of civil religion.

7. I'm glad you like to read. Guard your literacy and that of your children: thinking Christians, able to reason on the basis of God's Word, may become scarce in the future. Note how often St. Paul speaks of the mind, of wisdom, knowledge, understanding in his Epistles. We understand true doctrine with our minds, not with our feelings.

Your generation has reminded mine of the importance of feelings. I love to see radiant Christians, to be part of a group that "feels" the gospel. But I sometimes get uneasy about endless repetitions of simple phrases. Sing with your understanding as well as your feelings.

Remember that truth without feelings is still truth, but feelings without truth are at best mawkish, at worst heresy.

8. This one may surprise you, but I believe my generation's greatest loss—next to the inviolateness of marriage and the family—has been the sanctity of the Lord's Day. My wife and I started out our home with a rather serious attempt to "keep it

holy": no work, no group sports for our children, quiet activities, occasional visits with Christian friends and their children. But somewhere along the way we changed, and our attitude became much more secular (or pagan) than Christian—in the sense that I now believe the Bible teaches and our own parents and earlier generations practiced.

For yourself and for any children God may give you, try to recapture the Lord's Day as a day of rest and deeds of mercy, of retreat from the world; try to turn it into the happiest day of the week.

9. Be tolerant of different styles among Christians, different emphases. Remember that Jesus said, "He who is not against me is for me." Be intolerant of heresy—not of the right to speak; defend that with all your strength—but of accepting it as a viable option. Seek pure doctrine and life in the church, always remembering that "the wisdom that comes from above is first pure, then peaceable" (James 3:17).

10. If you see another person fall, help him up. And withhold judgment, at least that final kind reserved to the Judge of All that I think Jesus was referring to when he said, "Do not judge, and you will not be judged" (Luke 6:37).

And when you see somebody fall, let your first thought be, "That could have been me. It's only God's grace that enables me to stand."

11. Never forget that human beings are the most important creation in the world to God, and they should therefore be to you. Not just yourself, nor your family, nor other American Christians, but every other human being in the whole world. I think I can understand the concern of some people over endangered species: seals, whales, snail darters. But there are endangered humans, too: Amazon Indian tribes that may soon be extinct, Chicago inner-city kids, Cuban refugees, all created in the image of God. Give your life for men and women, teenagers, children—not for dollars or status.

Life is short, and every treasure on this earth will ultimately fail to satisfy the possessor: even a corner on the silver market or a Nobel or Pulitzer prize. So, in living your life, make your choices for God's glory and the good of others. The old divine's prayer is still a good one, "Oh God, burn eternity into my eyeballs."

When I was young, a couplet was often quoted:

> *Only one life, 'twill soon be past,*
> *Only what's done for Christ will last.*

It's still true.

# *Unlikely American Hero*

His lackluster resumé would never get beyond the church secretary's wastebasket, but ...

**July/August 1981**

It isn't likely he could serve on the board of most churches because he was a single young adult.

It isn't likely he'd be asked to speak at a liberated Christian women's conference because all his disciples were men.

It isn't likely he'd be asked to speak at a men's retreat because he cried publicly.

It isn't likely he'd pass most evangelism training courses because he adhered to no soul-winning formula and approached each person differently.

It isn't likely he could be the pastor of most churches because he said that people who remarry after divorce (except for marital unfaithfulness) are guilty of adultery.

It isn't likely he'd be asked to supply many pulpits because he often just told stories. And they were short.

It isn't likely he'd prepare Christian education materials because a lot of his stories were open-ended.

It isn't likely he could serve on a Christian college faculty because he drank wine.

It isn't likely he'd be asked to teach at a seminary because he had no earned doctorate and spent most of his time in practical work with his students.

It isn't likely he could serve on the board of a Christian institution or organization because he was poor.

It isn't likely he could preserve a reputation for leadership because he regularly took time out for rest and washed the feet of his followers.

It isn't likely he could be a counselor because he reinforced people's sense of sin, was directive, and turned from those who didn't respond.

It isn't likely he could run an electronic church because he told a rich man to give away his money to the poor, not to support his own ministry.

It isn't likely he could fill in at a youth conflicts seminar because he stood up to his parents when he was twelve (Luke 2:39–50), appealing to a higher responsibility, and refused to obey his mother when he was in his early thirties (John 2:1–4; Matt. 12:46–50).

It isn't likely he could fill in at most other seminars because he defined success in non-material terms.

It isn't likely he'd be used as an example of dying, because in his last hours he felt alienated from God the Father.

It isn't likely his opinion would be sought or heeded because he spoke of his followers in terms of a "little flock" and "two or three," warned against times when all men speak well of believers, and said that they should expect to be persecuted.

It isn't likely he'd expect people to come into church buildings; he'd probably be preaching in Central Park or the Boston Commons.

... If Jesus were here today.

Poor Church, poor world.

# *Walking Parables*

If Jeremiah were here today what would he say to the good guys?

**September 1981**

Jeremiah was in a hopeless situation, forced to declare God's impending judgment upon his own people, including their dispossession from their land.

To say that he was unpopular would be to deal with the prophet's situation lightly. His fellow townspeople, along with the king and almost everyone else, were out to kill him—even his family turned against him.

Then suddenly Jeremiah's life became a parable of hope when God told him to purchase a field. It was the field of Hanamel, his cousin—and it was in the very land from which God said their dispossession was imminent.

"We're going to return from captivity! I'm so sure of it that I'm investing in some real estate that will soon be abandoned." That was Jeremiah's message, unspoken but obvious, as he went through the legal technicalities of purchasing the field.

Reading that account in Jeremiah 32, I think of our Christian message to the world today . . . and the parable of our lives.

"Jesus is coming back!" is what we're saying. "We'll be taken out of this world when he returns and be transported to His Heavenly Kingdom. Others will go through great tribulation and eternal loss. No man knows the day or the hour, but there are signs of His coming soon: Israel is a nation now, there are wars and rumors of wars, earthquakes and other natural disasters, and various other signs."

We don't just share this message with ourselves; we tell the world that we are a people living among the doomed, in expectation of imminent rapture. We tell it on TV and radio programs, in films, on bumper stickers, in magazine articles and books. (One book—Hal Lindsey's *Late Great Planet Earth*—has sold 20 million copies.)

—Then our lives speak a most revealing parable. If Jesus is really our hope, if He's returning soon, people might expect us to be living rather modestly, spending our time and money in one last massive effort at evangelism and well-doing.

What do they see?

Christians who are as materialistic and hedonistic as anybody else in the American culture, Christians who have made financial success their god. Churches that are building bigger and bigger barns while the Third World starves for lack of bread, material, and living.

I remember, years ago, a poem lettered on the wall of McAuley-Cremorne Rescue Mission in New York—a poem that captured this disjuncture between professed belief and life:

> *Angels from their realms on high*
> *Look down on us with wondering eye,*
> *That where we are but passing guests,*
> *We build such strong and solid nests;*
> *But where we hope to dwell for aye,*
> *We scarce take heed one stone to lay.*

And they see other parables, related ones, in our lives.

Christians who present exalted teaching about marriage ("Love your wives as Christ also loved the church and gave himself for it" [Eph. 5:25]), then shed their wives and children as easily and without conscience as anyone else in our American culture.

I halfway understand the neighbor who finds that his wife has cancer and says, "I'll divorce her"; he's not Christian. I don't understand the Christian whose wife has an emotional breakdown, who divorces her, and leaves her with preteen children.

Aren't we scared to death that the Master of the house will return in the midst of our great big American Christian party of self-indulgence and demand an accounting of our stewardship? Or are we so hung up on Israel as a sign of His return that everything else is irrelevant?

Ah, Jeremiah, if you were here today, what would you say? How unpopular you would be in your own family.

# The Birth of an Ethic

## December 1981

*Behind Christmas 1981 exists a controversy that swirls around us like a winter storm*

Christmas 1981.

When did the fetus Jesus become a human being in Mary? When "He was conceived by the Holy Ghost," as the Apostles' Creed puts it, or at some later time during fetal development?

The controversy over pro-life, pro-freedom of choice, pro-abortion, anti-life, anti-abortion swirls around us like a winter storm.

I have some thoughts on the subject that probably will reflect my lay status in both medicine and theology. (Lay is frequently a synonym for ignorance.)

In all the discussion by pro- and anti-abortion activists, I have seen no reference to the fact that a criminal felony was changed into a permissible action overnight by a simple majority of the Supreme Court.

Prior to that decision, abortion (except for an abortion performed to save the life of the mother) was abhorred by almost everybody, including all Christians and most physicians.

It's hard for those of us who lived many years before that simple act of decriminalization to accept abortion's changed status. Imagine if infanticide or child abuse were suddenly declared legal. And we're puzzled by the medical community's immediate unquestioning acceptance, including that of many Christian physicians.

Those physicians are more likely to be obstetricians than pediatricians or orthopedists. I suppose the cynic in me comes to the surface when I ask why they were so ready to begin to abort pregnant women when the Court ruled it legal, although physicians resent any judicial impingement on other medical decisions? Was it the vast new source of income that suddenly opened up?

And the strident objections to cutting off government payment for abortions of poor women: was this caused by pity for the poor or by the loss of income? If the former, physicians are still free to abort poor women as a charitable act. I suspect few are thus aborted.

"The love of money is a root of all kinds of evil" (1 Tim. 6:10 NIV).

I understand that Christian theologians fall into two opinions about the origin of the soul in the fetus. First are those who believe the act of conception results in a living soul—a true, albeit embryonic, human being. Second are those who believe that sometime during the development of the fetus in the womb, God implants the soul. Nobody is sure when, but from that time on the fetus is not a "thing," but a human person.

Back to my first question: when did the fetal Jesus become a human being in Mary? From the Holy Spirit's conception, or later in its development?

And how about the fetal John's leap for joy when the sound of Mary's greeting reached his mother's ears? (Luke 1:41–44) Was that fetus a human being?

Canadian psychiatrist Thomas Verny has collected evidence, recently published in *The Secret Life of the Unborn Child* (Summit Books), that a fetus can feel emotion and respond intellectually months before birth. Item: a test shows that as early as twenty-five weeks a fetus will jump in time to the beat of an orchestra drum. It will grimace when sour liquids are injected into the amniotic sac, and double the rate of sucking when the liquid is sweet. Item: a mother in Oklahoma City discovers her one-year-old daughter reciting breathing instructions for Lamaze childbirth. But the terminology and technique are observably Canadian, not American. The mother had taken Lamaze while living in Toronto more than a year earlier.

This proves nothing; it does warn us to be careful about killing fetuses because they don't feel pain and aren't human.

One other question: could a not-yet-human inherit a sinful human nature? Yet David says, "Surely I have been a sinner from birth, sinful from the time my mother conceived me" (Ps. 51:5).

So it seems to me that I fall into the company of Christians who believe a fetus is human, a living soul, from the moment of conception.

One theologian suggested recently that for the second group (those who believe that at some point in time in utero the fetus becomes a living soul), abortion is defensible.

My son Tim, who has helped my thinking in this whole area of abortion, has a good answer for that.

"If a hunter is out looking for deer and sees something moving through the trees, he won't think it's either a deer or a human being and shoot. It's up to him to be sure it's a deer before he shoots, or he'll be in court for manslaughter.

"Isn't it logical that if we don't know exactly when a fetus becomes a living soul, a human being, we have no right to terminate its life on the chance that it may not be human yet?"

I am convinced that the legalization of abortion on demand has opened a Pandora's box of evil upon the United States, and that the silence of many Christians, especially Christian physicians, and churches is sinful—a condoning of evil.

Not speaking too strongly, Dr. R. G. Hammerton-Kelly, dean of chapel at Stanford University, put it this way: "In the time of Adolf Hitler—you must understand me, I know that arguments by historical analogy are very difficult—we do not ask of a church of that time, how was your singles' program? We do not ask of the church of that time, what was the quality, what was the intellectual quality of your preaching, how many books did your clergy produce? We ask only one thing: where did you stand when they led away your brothers and sisters? Where did you stand? Well, it is in those terms I'm afraid that I have come rather reluctantly to see this [abortion] issue."

—And I.

# Who Are We to Judge?

Is the Gate widening, or are we just not taking God's Word seriously anymore?

**November 1982**

A man who is separated from his wife writes a book that presents a new view of divorce—a view that permits it today for the same reason God permitted it in the Old Testament: the hardness of His people's hearts. The man is respected; the book is accepted. In fact it is welcomed by one of our most conservative evangelical periodicals, which headlines the review "Remarriage as God's Gift." Calling the book "monumental," the reviewer summarizes the new doctrine as "God's gracious action in permitting us to sin, then forgiving us and giving us another chance to succeed." And how many chances? Two, three, five?

Another man writes a book on how Christians should have a caring attitude toward others. He's divorced. Others continue in positions of leadership, including youth work, after divorce and remarriage.

The reviewer of the book I alluded to earlier says that "evangelical thinking about divorce has been cast in concrete since the early 50s, with the works of John Murray, Guy Duty, and Charles Ryrie forming the basic framework for that thinking." I wonder why he only went back thirty years instead of to Jesus' teaching in the New Testament. Surely Christian thinking about divorce was cast in concrete then and continued until ten or fifteen years ago when evangelical Christians discovered that divorce with remarriage was acceptable. Subsequently new and exciting (or comforting) discoveries were made by so-called theologians to rationalize the disdain of Christians for the teachings of the Bible.

A similar pattern is displayed in liberation theology, women's theology, black theology, homosexual theology. Maybe I shouldn't lump these together; I am not implying that some of them don't have valid, biblical goals. But they are alike in starting with a problem, a need, a desire, rather than with God; then building a construct that is unbalanced, to support their teaching about that need. If Bible passages have to be explained away or even rejected to support their thesis, so be it.

I remember studying under C. T. Craig, New Testament scholar and Revised Standard Version translator at Union Seminary the summer of 1942. The course was "The Pauline Interpretation of the Gospel." For the first few weeks Dr. Craig could not have been more clear in his understanding of the Pauline teaching if he had been teaching at Dallas or Wheaton.

Then, at a critical point in the course, he said, "Up to this time we've been studying what Paul actually said. Now we shall proceed to reinterpret his writings in the light of the twentieth century." From then on he cut down what he had previously built. St. Paul was "a child of his times"; cultural change necessitated drastic revision of his ideas.

I could not have been persuaded in 1942 that forty years later a respected professor at an evangelical seminary would reject St. Paul's teaching about gender differences with almost the same words.

How far we've strayed from believing and obeying the Word of God.

The evangelical church is sick—so sick that people are crowding in to join us. We're a big flock, big enough to permit remarriage of divorced people (beyond the exception Jesus allowed), big enough to permit practicing homosexuals to pursue their lifestyle, big enough to tolerate almost anything pagans do. We're no longer narrow; it's the wide road of popular acceptance for us.

185

"When the Son of Man cometh, shall he find faith on the earth?" (Luke 18:8).

That question asked by our Lord haunts me. To me its implications are far more serious than the timetable of His return, over which we spend so much time arguing.

What do I suggest?

First, that we begin to take the Bible seriously again, as God's Word—God's Word. Not something to hold conferences about, to give lip service to; something to reckon with and to obey.

If we take the Bible seriously, we won't rationalize the parts that convict us of sin—whether the sin of divorce and remarriage, the sin of homosexual relations, the sin of scorning the poor, or the sin of genocide by nuclear weapons.

Somehow we must restore the sacredness of the marriage vows. Maybe there could be two different ceremonies; one for those who have foresworn divorce and remarriage; another for those who consider divorce and remarriage an option "if this doesn't work out." I'd like to see all latter such ceremonies relegated to the county clerk's office.

By revealing my thoughts, by writing these words and submitting them to the editor for publication, I have stepped away seemingly from the tolerant, caring, loving, "who am I to judge?" attitude of many evangelicals, including many of my friends. I'm considered judgmental; I ought to cast the beam out of my own eye (Matt. 7:3–5); I've forgotten to show love; I'm getting old.

To those who consider the latter a valid objection, especially since I've been married to the same person for thirty-nine years, I'd like to say that pressures on marriage are nothing new. Don't think my generation and previous generations were free from the relational, emotional, financial, health, and spiritual problems— including the temptation to commit adultery—that confront you today. We were confronted; some of us had good marriages, some poor ones.

But divorce wasn't an "out" for previous generations of Christians. Maybe that was the reason we honored our promise to stick to our mate for life, "until death us do part."

I like to think that a lot of us were persuaded that we'd made the best choice in the whole world and that nobody else (including young flesh) could be better. And I like to think that we had a bit more concern for our children.

# A Child's Heart

Is the issue of divorce the church's acid-test for words like love, compassion, and obedience?

**May 1983**

My November column ("Who Are We to Judge," about the growing rate and rationalization of divorce in our evangelical churches) brought the largest number of responses of any column in recent years. Most of them expressed agreement with my comments on the changing attitude toward ending marriage and, in a larger sense, not taking the Scriptures seriously.

Two letters reveal differing points of view. Here's the first:

> My reaction to the article is one of deep compassion for the angry, frightened, threatened person who wrote it.
>
> The first question has to be: What deep-seated fear drives him to his attitude and position about divorce and remarriage? And more specifically, about those of us who are divorced? Perhaps it would be worth his while to take himself and his article to a good Christian psychiatrist. The article could hold the key to understanding some serious underlying emotional problem.
>
> Bayly mentions the need to take God's Word seriously. By that I assume he means I should interpret it as he does. To me, taking God's Word seriously means to seek to know and understand what God means and what his intentions are, in an honest way. While Bayly and I may never agree about what God is saying in his Word about divorce and remarriage, it is

almost impossible to misunderstand what he is saying about love, compassion, forgiveness, and acceptance. I believe God extends these things to those of us who are divorced as well as to liars, thieves, murderers, junkies, whoremongers, elders, deacons, pastors, Christian magazine editors, et al.

Certainly the vituperation and the almost hysterical condemnation that characterize this article do not demonstrate the love we are commanded to have for one another. If it does, please don't love me anymore! . . .

The other letter has a different tone:

Thank you for saying that. I am separated from my wife of [many] years and lately have been very close to taking divorce action. She just has not acknowledged me as her husband for a long while and though the pain has subsided after [a number of] months' separation, there is still such tension and strain, even in my continuing contact with our kids, that I've nearly fallen prey to the thinking that to divorce would be the thing. Few Christians have tried to dissuade me from this thinking. The pastor of our family's church—where I no longer attend—brought up the subject in our last phone conversation, knowing that in our state we have now fulfilled the time required for granting a "no-fault" divorce.

But I have been arrested by the plain teaching of the Word and have renewed my commitment not to divorce, and to seek for the reuniting of our family. The latter looks impossible, and I need two things, as I see it—a heart united in believing that what is obviously God's best will may be done, and a new love for [my wife],

But your call to us to return to the Scripture's teaching is what I—and many like me—need. We are weak enough. Without the Word, which I am studying on a daily basis, I would have washed out long ago. I can easily see why others do so with little thought or hope . . .

Separation hurts. Divorce hurts. The hurt—which I haven't experienced—is apparent in both letters.

God's Word also hurts. And, as the great missionary to India's women and children, Amy Carmichael, wrote, "If you have never been hurt by a word from God, it is probable that you have never heard God speak."

A dear child wrote the following psalm and gave it to me at Christmas. At the top of the page on which it's written is a carefully drawn cross:

> *Please forgive me.*
> *Please forgive me.*
> *O please.*
> *I've done wrong and*
> *I love you so much*
> *I just can't leave you.*

Tender is the heart of a child. Tender toward God, tender toward sin.

We adults need that tenderness. It can be ours, as shown by the second letter from which I've quoted. This example of faithfulness to a commitment to God and a partner, and determination to seek reconciliation, means a great deal in such a time as this. I admire the man who wrote it.

And I hope the child's heart remains tender. I pray that it will.

# *No Room in the Seminary*

## December 1983

*Jesus was a "blue collar" worker before His ministry. How far have we strayed from His method of training His Twelve?*

I was having lunch with an unusually qualified pastor, one who at about fifty-five years of age has spent thirty years in the Christian ministry.

"What would you do with the rest of your career if you could choose any area of service?" I asked.

"Teach in a seminary," he replied. "But that's not a live option. I don't have a union card—and believe me, seminaries have powerful unions to keep out anyone who doesn't possess a Ph.D."

Here's a man of extraordinary proven gifts and experience, a man who has ministered to steel workers in the East, farmers in California, a Christian college community, a major university community. And his wife is equally gifted.

Yet he is excluded from sharing lifetime lessons and experience because he doesn't belong to the "Ph.D. union."

My friends will know that this situation is no new concern to me. For many years I have said that one huge problem in the Church is that in preparing men and women for ministry we have followed the Roman Catholic pattern of scholastic training rather than Jesus' training of the Twelve. About the only way we've followed His example is in the three-year training period.

Those are hard words, but they represent a conviction forged over a lifetime, reinforced in recent years by my firsthand experience with three sons in one of the best evangelical seminaries.* (I realize that I will not help the two who remain— one is now the minister of two small churches—by what I write.)

The closest parallel I can find is in medical school education. What if medical students never observed a skilled surgeon perform surgery, never went on rounds with a skilled internist, but only learned from books and lectures?

I must immediately issue a disclaimer. Many seminary professors do take interim part-time pastorates, in addition to their normal teaching duties. But this is no real substitute for the day-in, day-out experiences of a pastor, rescue mission director, Christian education director, evangelist, or other worker.

In many seminaries, professors of homiletics (sermon preparation and preaching) have never had the grueling and wondrous

---
*Gordon-Conwell Theological Seminary.

experience of preparing three different messages a week for forty-eight weeks each year, year after year.

Andrew Blackwood was the dean of homiletics professors when he taught at Princeton Seminary. I don't think he had an earned doctorate; regardless, he only came to Princeton after years of experience in local churches. It was Blackwood who trained most of the great Presbyterian preachers of my generation.

How did Jesus train the disciples in homiletics? By His own modeling; they were present at the Sermon on the Mount, on occasions when He confronted an angry group, at small gatherings.

They learned counseling by observing Him counsel.

Even their insights into Scripture were molded by His public teaching and informal teaching of the Twelve.

I do not question the value, even the necessity of learning Hebrew and New Testament Greek, church history, Bible, and other seminary subjects. I do suggest that even these should not be lectures isolated from lives involved in service.

If we follow Jesus' example, the New Testament professor would also be the person who has a prison ministry, in which he trains students by their own involvement. The Old Testament professor might exercise skills (probably with his or her spouse) in children's work—perhaps seaside summer missions.

I do not believe professors in our evangelical seminaries are much different in their teaching methods and in modeling for their students than professors in university graduate schools. In fact, students in medicine and some sciences probably have more involvement in their professors' work.

Someone may ask, "Where can you find such a combination of skills?"

There are at least two answers to this. One friend of mine is a most capable Greek teacher; he has taught Greek at one of our top Christian colleges. He has a great wife. They have had missionary experience in Hong Kong and South America. Would a seminary hire him, with such a combination of skills and experience? Unfortunately, no; he doesn't possess the Ph.D. union card.

So by looking—if seminaries were not encumbered with

"trade union" restrictions—such people would be available in many fields.

Another answer is to develop such combinations, even among Ph.D.s. (I do not derogate the value of graduate study; I do question its becoming a requirement to train God's servants. I also question the subjects chosen for many dissertations and the depth of research required.)

Instead of encouraging bright students to remain on the academic continuum, then return to teach after several years of graduate study, it might be wiser to say, "Take a church. Get seven years in the pastorate under your belt, then come back and teach." Or missionary service, student work—even, for some who have been unusually sheltered, secular employment. (We must never forget that Jesus was a blue collar worker for many years before He began His "career" in teaching.)

In some parts of the seminary curriculum, the skill itself should be practiced before the person assays to teach others. Christian education is one of those areas where there is no substitute for experience.

A seminary once asked me to suggest a candidate for a vacancy in its Christian education department. I suggested a man I consider one of the most capable, experienced Christian educators in the country. The man I recommended has had more experience in the field than anyone else I know; youth work in one of America's finest churches; supervision of C.E. programs in another, along with Christian school oversight; C.E. and administration in an inner-city church, the same in the largest church in its denomination; all in different parts of the United States, and he was then under fifty.

He was turned down, to the students' great loss. Why? He had no union card.

If the system is in place so solidly that even the seminary trustees cannot or will not change it for the good of both students and churches, I have two suggestions, one conservative, the other radical.

Before making them, I should mention that there's a movement among some Conservative Baptist pastors for their seminaries to require a year's internship before awarding a degree. So far, the seminaries have not been enthusiastic about the proposal, citing increased costs.

My first suggestion, then, the conservative one: Appoint experienced but not-holding-a-union-card men and women to "in residence" professorial status. Provide housing on or near the seminary property so the pastor, missionary, student worker, or other person in residence could have an extended ministry beyond the classroom. I have a hunch that churches or missionary societies would gladly give up the likes of Chuck Swindoll or Clayton Bell for a semester or two for such a strategic ministry. They might even pay his salary.

At Pennsylvania State University a few years ago they had the George Westinghouse Chair of Industrial Engineering. An executive of Westinghouse Company was appointed full professor for a two-year period, with the company continuing him on its payroll. The two-year limitation was to prevent the professor from growing stale in industrial techniques, becoming an ivory tower scholastic.

My second, more radical, suggestion is to turn a couple of seminaries into discipleship schools with close contact between teachers and students, shared ministries and homes (remember how important Martin Luther's "table talk" was for younger men?), and perhaps even summer projects in Christian work in logging camps, unchurched areas, seashore resorts, prison ministry.

Or if no seminaries can be changed, start some new ones. Seminaries that declare themselves open shops from the very beginning, and stick to it.

—A seminary in which Jesus, the Apostle Peter, Dwight L. Moody, Billy Graham, or Francis Schaeffer could teach.

# Our Reich of Indifference
## June 1984

*We castigate the apathy of Christians in Nazi Germany—and ignore our own silence on today's holocaust of abortion.*

There is a sin of indifference. It is the sin that binds evangelicals as the Lilliputians bound Gulliver, preventing us from exercising the influence that God has given us in these years—years that are destined to come to an end and may never be repeated.

To me, the outstanding example of indifference is in our reaction to the great sin of abortion that is the shame of our nation. Each year, one-and-a-half million humans who bear the image of God are murdered, many, perhaps most of them, with accompanying great pain to which a group of non-Christian physicians recently attested. The pain is that of poisoning by a saline solution or dismemberment, being torn apart and removed in pieces from the uterus. (In the latter part of the second and in the third trimester, this is now the procedure of choice, since it removes the possibility of delivering a viable infant.)

Many Americans who protest Canada's annual seal hunt, in which baby seals are clubbed to death, are the most vociferous in defending a mother's right to have her not-yet-born child killed, with greater pain than the baby seals suffer.

We Christians are indifferent. After all, the Supreme Court of the United States by an eight-member majority condemned these millions to death (by some estimates, 17 million since Roe v. Wade in 1973). As good Christian citizens we accept this as the law of the land.

Our Christian physicians will be judged for their indifference. With notable exceptions the United States medical establishment, including Christians, has been silent about our great national sin.

Why this silence?

According to Father John Powell, Roman Catholic Spokesman for the anti-abortion movement, the answer is money. "I have heard many doctors say that even if the Supreme Court reverses Roe v. Wade and declares abortions illegal, they will continue to perform them. I have never heard a doctor say that he will continue to perform abortions if he is not paid for them."

We blame Christians in Germany during the Third Reich for their indifference to the murder of Jews. "Why were you silent?" we ask.

Someday we will be asked the same question. And a righteous God will not judge the German nation without also judging our nation.

Ironically, in 1975 (two years after our own Supreme Court's decision that a fetus is not a person) Western Germany's Federal Constitutional (Supreme) Court firmly stated the unborn child's right to life. Thus the heirs of the Third Reich alone among Western nations that ruled on abortion statutes during a two-year period (United States, Austria, France, Italy, Western Germany, and Canada) affirmed the historic, Judeo-Christian position.

Why are we silent, indifferent to the anti-abortion movement? (I prefer this to pro-life, just as I'd have preferred an anti-gas oven movement in Germany to a pro-Jewish life movement. We like to turn horrible matters into more pleasant positive statements.)

One reason for our indifference, I believe, is the silence of our preachers. Few are crying out against this great evil, pronouncing judgment on a nation of killers. "After all, we don't want to make a young woman in the congregation who has had an abortion feel guilty."

Maybe a woman should face up to the fact that her action has destroyed a human life—a life totally independent of her own—that is growing within her.

I think another reason is that our priorities are skewed. We emphasize growth in the congregation's size, new buildings, exciting programs; these are the test of our effectiveness. Yet how we'd scorn a German Christian who said, "Let me tell you about the new building we put up and paid for during 1938-40," or "We had such a great singles' program."

Still another reason is the identification many make of the American government, including the Supreme Court, with the Kingdom of God, or at least an Old Testament theocracy. The lines have been blurred between God and Caesar. We have a knee-jerk reaction that Caesar's degree is morally and ethically right; this determines our evangelical ideas of morality and spirituality. We're really convinced that God is only concerned about personal morality, and that only as it is related to narrow areas of life. Let the state handle the big issues.

In 1948 I was in Europe for a Christian student camp. One night we were discussing the recently ended war. The group of ten included French, British, and German students, all of whom, except for me, had seen active duty. A German student told about the crucial experience that stood out for him. He had taken a stand against dancing. (Afterward another German student, from the same small evangelical denomination, said he had taken the same stand.)

"I ruined my chances for officers training," the German student said, "because I refused to participate in social dances, which was required of officers. But I had been brought up, in home and church, to believe that dancing is wrong."

" 'Dancing is wrong'—but what did they teach you about the murder of Jews?" I remember how the thought raced through my mind. Perhaps to my shame, but out of concern for Christian unity and peace in the cabin, I didn't say it aloud.

Are we giving moral training to the teens and young adults—and older adults—in our evangelical churches? Or are we silent as government and television train them—while we're satisfied to guard them from dancing and other similar perils to the soul?

God, forgive our indifference. Make us burn with white heat against injustice, especially the destruction of the weak and totally vulnerable, who bear your divine image.

# The Power of Negative Thinking

What form of godliness are "pre-evangelists" like Schuller preaching?

**July/August 1984**

About forty years ago, when I was in seminary, I was bothered by the praise my parents gave Norman Vincent Peale for his radio ministry. They listened to him faithfully, along with Charles E. Fuller, of "The Old Fashioned Revival Hour." They also contributed money to support the programs.

With the theological acumen of a seminary student, I objected, "But he never mentions sin, he doesn't try to bring people to Christ. His preaching just makes you feel good."

—To which they (especially Mother) simply replied that they got blessings from Dr. Peale, whether I could understand it or not. And he was a Christian and believed the same as we did.

I finally gave up trying to dissuade them because the argument was ruining every visit home. But I had one final word.

"You know, you're both Christians, and you put Christian content into his preaching. You hear him with all your preconceptions about sin and salvation. But what about people who aren't Christians?"

These memories are stirred by several recent publications. First was an interview with Dr. Peale published Easter Sunday in *Family Weekly*. The interviewer was James S. Kunen. Here's the part that disturbed me, just like my mother did while I was in seminary.

> "I'm Jewish," [Kunen said,] "and in your book you talk about putting all your faith in Jesus. Does that leave me out?"
>
> "I'm so glad you brought that up!" he replied with genuine enthusiasm. "When you run into 'Jesus,' just change

it to 'God.'" He gazed into the distance, reflecting. "This teaches me another lesson, maybe. I write for everybody; maybe I'd better use 'God' more and 'Jesus' less. But when I do that, I get a feeling of being disloyal."

"You could just say once at the beginning of your next book what you've said to me," I suggested.

"You think that would cover it?"

"I think that would do it."

"Except, we would get thousands of letters," Ruth [Peale] cautioned him.

"It's true that there are an awful lot of narrow-minded people in the world," Dr. Peale agreed.

The second publication was *New England Church Life* (incidentally, an outstanding regional publication). Dr. Robert Schuller had recently spoken at Gordon-Conwell Theological Seminary, and had faced some of the same questions I asked my mother many years ago. Debra P. Davis reported on Dr. Schuller's message and the response.

> [After asserting his orthodox Christian beliefs], Schuller defended his TV ministry by pointing out that he is trying to reach the "unchurched, secular people" and he finds that the way to change these people is by "telling them they are what you wish they would become. People do not need to be told they are sinners," he added, "they already know that."

What was the response of these latter-day seminarians?

> One student struggled with accepting all that she heard, wondering if she was biased or had good reasons for concern. "It's as if I have a cloud inside. I'm not sure why," she deliberated.
>
> Another knew exactly where he stood. David Currie, noting that the doctrine of sin is "conspicuously absent" from Schuller's preaching, said, "He only seems to present half the issue, passing over sin and the need for repentance."

The final publication that took me back in memory forty years was Robert Schuller's recent book, *Tough Times Never Last, But Tough People Do!* (Nelson).

Dr. Schuller has written this book primarily for the unemployed in these hard economic times. It is to a considerable extent autobiographical and tells about the growth of his ministry and assorted properties.

Since I had just read the interview with Dr. Peale in *Family Weekly*, I noticed that Dr. Schuller almost invariably refers to "God" and "Lord." He does refer to Jesus at least four times: he mentions a tornado on his father's farm that left unharmed a molded plaster motto, "Keep looking to Jesus"; in another reference, he says: "Everyone has within him some idea of something that he should have started but hasn't. Maybe it's to quit smoking. Maybe it's to lose weight. Maybe it's to get started on a physical fitness program. Maybe it's to join a church. Maybe it's to accept Jesus Christ as your Savior and Lord. Maybe it's to read the Bible, which you never have done. Maybe it's to start a new business."

What's my present thinking about Drs. Peale and Schuller?

First, I'm sure they help many, many people to cope with difficult lives; middle and upper income people who need positive reinforcement. Most preachers probably don't provide this. My own parents appreciated it from Dr. Peale.

Second, this encouragement is basically to trust oneself and one's inherent possibilities, not to trust God. I'm sure they'd both disagree with this, but I don't think you can read their writings or listen to them without coming to this conclusion. Some people—like my parents—fit this into their orthodox Christian beliefs.

Third, in the case of Dr. Schuller at least, a different, thoroughly evangelical ministry is carried on at his church, Crystal Cathedral. There's no doubt where the church stands in spite of the dog and pony shows (their Easter extravaganza cost $1 million to produce.)

Fourth (and this is very important), some preachers may be called to a ministry of pre-evangelism. I'm not saying that Peale and Schuller haven't been God's instruments in bringing people to the new birth, but—unlike Billy Graham—this isn't their primary ministry.

These are confusing days in the United Sates. Maybe God is

building $20 million church edifices and $30 million electronic church motels. Maybe conviction of sin and repentance aren't related to salvation any longer. Maybe people need the success and prosperity theme to bring them to Christ. Maybe not.

To be sure would be terrifying for any American Christian who gets beyond dollars and numbers to the spiritual condition of church and society.

# The End of an Era

## October 1985

*Remember that the greatest strides in Christianity's history—the first century church—were taken when the church had no money or property.*

**M**y generation of evangelical Christians is in the process of passing the torch to the next generation. Thus it has always been in the church; thus it will always be until our Lord returns.

The end of World War II brought a fresh impetus to Christian activity and leadership in this country. Our torch-passing forty years later therefore represents a more distinct period of time than many other less clearly defined transitions in the past. It is the end of an era.

This is a good time to consider the inheritance we received from those who passed the torch to us, and the inheritance we are bequeathing to those who will stand for evangelical principles and serve our Lord during the next forty years.

Editor's Note: This month Joseph Bayly begins his twenty-fifth year of writing "Out of My Mind"

If I were to suggest a broad generalization, it would be that we were pioneers and our successors are the settlers.

I write as an observer of the evangelical scene, a participant in some of the movements. Many of my contemporaries will see things differently; they may be right and I may be wrong. But here are my impressions, my interim report on the stewardship exercised by my generation.

I present this report in terms of what we received from our predecessors, including our children.

## Storefronts and Liberals

We inherited a religious scene dominated by liberals; we bequeath liberalism in shambles.

We inherited a Berlin Wall between evangelical Christians and Roman Catholics; we bequeath a spirit of love and rapprochement on the basis of the Bible rather than fear and hatred.

We inherited 11,000 overseas missionaries; we bequeath 40,000.

We inherited a Church torn by strife and schism. We bequeath a Church in which healing and reunion have taken place.

We inherited a reputation for anti-intellectualism; we bequeath a generation of scholars and scholarly work.

We inherited aging church buildings, plus some storefronts and roofed-over basements—construction started but interrupted by the Great Depression. As a result of the biggest church-building boom in history, we bequeath a treasure of up-to-date properties and facilities.

We inherited a handful of poor, struggling Christian colleges. We bequeath a score of accredited institutions of higher education.

We inherited three or four small independent seminaries; we bequeath nine or ten healthy institutions that are the major source of trained evangelical leadership for America's churches and parachurch movements.

We inherited one national youth movement—Christian Endeavor, working through the local church—and a Sunday evening young people's meeting, often attended by adults. We bequeath a sophisticated understanding of teens and young adults applied within the local church and outside the church by thousands of professionals. Parachurch youth organizations we founded include Youth for Christ, Young Life, Inter-Varsity Christian Fellowship, and Campus Crusade for Christ.

In other areas of the churches' concern, we inherited denominational, church-centered programs for children, youth and adults. We bequeath Child Evangelism Fellowship, Christian Service Brigade, Pioneer Ministries, Christian Business Men's Committee, Bible Study Fellowship, Neighborhood Bible Studies, Christian Medical Society, Christian Legal Society, Nurses Christian Fellowship, and many other parachurch programs.

We inherited *Christian Herald* and the *Sunday School Times*, rather quaint magazines with limited circulation, that looked shabby next to *Time* or the *Saturday Evening Post*. We bequeath more than a hundred periodicals with a circulation of many millions that don't look strange next to the secular magazines on the coffee table.

We inherited scattered local radio programs, while the rest of religious radio—except for Charles E. Fuller's "Old Fashioned Revival Hour"—was monopolized by the National Council of Churches. We bequeath an end to the monopoly (and the National Council's power), innumerable local radio and television programs, several networks, many independent stations, and an electronic church that takes in $500 million dollars a year.

We inherited camp and conference facilities that were as primitive as the motels of those earlier days. We bequeath many more camps and conferences, as modern as today's resorts, with professional leadership.

We inherited a few publishers and several hundred bookstores. We bequeath a hundred publishers and five thousand bookstores.

Looking at that list, I wonder at all that God has done through his weak, failing people during the past forty years. "This is the Lord's doing; it is marvelous in our eyes" (Ps. 118:23).

But the bequests are not all good.

*Success Here and Now*

We inherited the integrity of marriage and the family; we bequeath a new permissiveness toward divorce and a new pattern of single-parent families.

We inherited a clearly defined, biblical value system; we bequeath shattered values.

We inherited belief in the humanness of unborn babies and the criminality of murdering them in the uterus. We bequeath an unending American Holocaust of 19 million corpses, increasing at the rate of 1.5 million a year. We also bequeath a general unconcern among evangelical Christians.

We inherited doctrinal, expository preaching with a heavy emphasis on prophecy. We bequeath relational preaching with a heavy emphasis on success here and now.

We inherited leaders who spoke out against evil in society and the Church; we bequeath leaders who are specialists in public relations and fundraising.

We inherited a four-week Daily Vacation Bible School; we bequeath one-week schools or the end of D.V.B.S.

We inherited deep distrust of commercial entertainment, typified by sanctions against movie-going. We bequeath acceptance of every kind of entertainment in the living room, available to children. (But we also bequeath a Christian entertainment industry.)

We inherited Christians who were loyal to their church, consistent in their living, and restrained in talking about their faith. We bequeath Christians who are loyal to many religious organizations in addition to—sometimes in preference to—their church, who are less concerned about consistent living, and who have been taught to talk constantly about their faith.

We inherited homes and churches that were patriarchal, overseas missions that were to a large extent matriarchal. We bequeath an unsolved problem of reconciling the Bible with cultural change in the role of women.

We inherited the Lord's Day as a day of rest. We bequeath a completely secularized Sunday.

We inherited family togetherness and activities; we bequeath age-level activities and small groups in the church.

We inherited government friendly toward the Church and a Church uninvolved in government. We bequeath government hostile toward the Church and the Church enmeshed in politics and civil religion.

## We Cannot Program God

What do I think the agenda for the new generation of leaders should be?

It may surprise you, but I don't think an agenda is advisable, even possible, for the evangelical Christian movement.

Looking at my list of positive bequests above, I'm impressed with the lack of long-range planning shown by the various developments.

Certainly there was little inter-relatedness among them, except that one person's step of faith encouraged another to exercise similar faith. Or it may be more accurate to say that the Holy Spirit's blessing in certain areas led to expectations of like blessing in others.

For instance, Jim Rayburn and Stacey Woods were at small Dallas Seminary at the same time. Rayburn's success with high school kids may have led Woods to undertake a university movement. And the recent risk taken by the founders of that seminary may have affected both of them.

In a similar manner, a rash of overseas missionary societies arose after World War II. (Servicemen had been exposed to foreign cultures and observed at firsthand the needs.) Each new society encouraged others to take the plunge.

We cannot program the Holy Spirit. Where He wills, He works.

We also cannot program such factors as the economy, government, taxes, and public—or Christian—response.

The public may turn on evangelical Christianity, especially if government policies supported by evangelicalism's self-appointed spokesmen fail. The government may become increasingly hostile toward the Church, private Christian colleges, and other institutions.

Taxation may force us to sell many of our properties. There is no guarantee against persecution by the time the new generation stands with the forty-year perspective from which I write—in the year 2025.

Rather than an agenda, I suggest several attitudes to our heirs based on our experience.

## Fresh Risks; Old Faith

Don't avoid risks. You are settlers rather than pioneers; therefore the risks may be different—and greater. The ramifications of making a wrong decision increase as the organization grows. More is at stake. But risk is a concomitant of faith.

Watch out for a temptation to consider the universe as within the province of your organization. I see this tendency already in organizations which started out with a specific objective: Navigators, Inter-Varsity Christian Fellowship, Campus Crusade for Christ, and electronic churches, for instance.

Attempts at monopoly are even more dangerous in Christian work than in secular business. An effective money machine may be Satan's provision rather than the Holy Spirit's direction.

Constantly aim at increasing the degree of lay involvement, even if it means cutting down the number of professional workers. Lay persons, if trained, have an "in" that professionals usually lack. Further, if the time comes when professionals are excluded because of government decree or lack of financing, lay persons can carry on the work.

Guard the doctrinal and spiritual integrity that has been bequeathed to you. Keep the faith with previous generations in this area above all others.

Institutions, like individuals, grow middle—and old—aged. Avoid this not only by taking fresh risks, but by trusting younger leadership.

Rather than increasing organization/institutional lands and goods, ask what you can do without, what alternatives exist to the expenditure of funds for capital growth. Good stewards do not dream up ways to spend money just because the money machine can produce it. Remember that the greatest strides in Christianity's history—the first century church—were taken when the Church was unencumbered by money and property. Maybe, just maybe, there's an organization somewhere that will say to its constituency, "We're satisfied with our headquarters building, the size of our staff. Yes, we're a bit crowded and could use more space; yes, we could figure out where to place more staff. But give your money to digging wells and sending agriculturists to Africa.

In this passing of the torch, this changing of the guard, I commend you to the God of all grace, the never-changing One. May He give you grace, wisdom, humility, and courage.

When the Nazis invaded the Netherlands, some villagers asked the local medical doctor what they should do.

"Before the invading army we must be as lions," he replied, "before God as worms."

Great advice.

# *Rome Fell While Moralists Slept*
## January 1986

*Like environmentalists fighting for laws for clean air, we have the right to fight for laws against moral pollution.*

Y ou can't legislate morality" has become the battle cry of libertarians in recent years whenever Christians have forsaken their trenches and spoken up for moral principles as a basis for civil laws.

Abortion, homosexuality, pornography—even prostitution—have been defended against any attack with those words.

Sadly, many Christians have accepted the argument and

become silent about these evils. So the trenches are full of sleeping moralists, and victory has been won by fighting libertarians.

You may not be able to legislate morality, but our country has certainly legislated its approval of immorality. (This seems to me to be a close parallel to the total exclusion of Christian religion from public schools and the total freedom of expression given to advocates of agnostic religion—some call it secular humanism.)

And so we have seen homosexuality and abortion decriminalized during the past twenty years. Prostitution is legal in much of Nevada. Only child sexual abuse and pornography—though on public display, even in neighborhood convenience stores—are illegal. Even here libertarians are fighting for the right of adults to introduce children to sexual experience. Attacks on laws against incest are frequent. After all, we're told, with new birth control methods the danger of genetic anomalies is practically eliminated, so what's the harm. "You can't legislate morality in the home, of all places."

Besides, why should Christians force their moral ideas on the whole population through laws? Here's why.

1. We believe that there is such a thing as moral pollution, a climate of decadence that characterized Rome and other civilizations in their declining years. As good citizens we have the right—even the responsibility—to fight for laws that will prohibit prostitution, pornography, abortion, homosexuality, and other evils. We have the responsibility to provide a safe moral climate for our children and grandchildren to grow up in. This right is as clear as that of environmentalists to fight for laws that will insure clean air, water, and soil for present and future generations.

2. There are public consequences of the private acts of "consenting adults." A prime example of this is AIDS. Open sewers lead to typhoid epidemics; homosexual practices have led to the AIDS epidemic.

I'm troubled when I read statistics that are aimed at exonerating homosexuals for the AIDS epidemic. Users of contaminated needles, hemophiliacs, and heterosexuals—not just homosexuals—are spreading the fatal disease, we're told. But where does the virus come from that infects those innocent parties—even babies? Homosexuals. That there should be any question about closing public bathhouses in New York or San Francisco, places where homosexuals engage in promiscuous sex, angers me. This is as much a matter of public health as prohibiting drainage of sewage into our cities' gutters.

Further, we Christians are paying for the epidemic homosexuals have introduced with our tax and health-insurance dollars. No one has come forward with statistics related to the escalating cost of this disease. This would seem harsh and unsympathetic toward sufferers, as do my words. Sympathy and understanding have become prime virtues in our society. Do any citizens, including Christians, have the right to object to the decriminalization of a lifestyle that carries such heavy costs in human tragedy and economic loss?

3. From a Christian standpoint (but remember that Christians are also citizens of a democracy), we cannot escape the words of Jesus Christ about nations being judged. The United States is our nation as surely as Germany during the Third Reich was German Christians' nation. Silence before the slaughter of Jews, silence before the slaughter of the unborn; either one, we believe, lays us open to the judgment of God. Therefore we have a duty to influence legislation and the courts by our murmurings, or thunderings, and voting.

4. The prohibition of alcohol in the twenties is usually the example used to prove the dictum, "You can't legislate morality." I'm not sure Prohibition was really a "noble experiment" that failed. It failed with the sophisticated and wealthy; I'm not sure it failed equally with the poor and middle class.

Regardless, I'd prefer the abolition of slavery rather than Prohibition as an example of moral change brought about by Christians. Nobody calls the war that brought freedom to slaves a holy war. Yet that freedom was a direct result of Christian intransigence in the face of a great social evil, a moral blot on our nation.

The writings of Jonathan Blanchard, first president of Wheaton College, reveal this intransigence, this unwillingness to accept half a loaf. In fact, he scorned any sort of compromise with slave holders.

We have become a compromising Christian community to such an extent that we are now compromised. We invite proponents of "evangelical" practicing homosexuality to speak at our training institutions and sacred assemblies. We seriously propose compromise on the abortion issue rather than excise the evil.

You can't legislate morality? Tell that to William Wilberforce, or to William Lloyd Garrison. It will have to be in heaven, unfortunately, when we're rationalizing our own inaction toward the evils of our times. "Had we lived then," we'll say, "we'd have stood with you."

Jesus said it: We dedicate memorials to dead prophets and kill living ones on our way home from the cemetery (Matt. 23:29–34).

# *The Happy Healer*

## June 1986

*We American Christians are as anxious to avoid dying as any of our contemporaries.*

For years I've been intrigued by Jesus' words, "I tell you, my friends, do not be afraid of those who kill the body and after that can do no more" (Luke 12:4 NIV).

"All they can do is kill you." If we had not been raised in Sunday school and church, those words heard without the familiarity that breeds shallowness, would shock us. What's to be feared more than death, especially death by murder or execution, death at the whim of another that terminates all relationships and pleasures, cuts short our careers, ends all our plans?

But most of us do have a Christian background, so we place those words in a familiar context along with Daniel entering the lion's den, John the Baptist's head on a platter, Stephen stoned by a mob, Jesus crucified. The words are true; they've been proven true by men and women in the biblical past.

So we sing,

> *A glorious band, the chosen few*
> *On whom the Spirit came,*
> *Twelve valiant saints, their hope they knew,*
> *And mocked the cross and flame;*
> *They met the tyrant's brandished steel,*
> *The lion's gory mane;*
> *They bowed their necks the stroke to feel;*
> *Who follows in their train?*

—Who does follow in their train? Russian and Chinese Christians, of course. We thank God for modern Christians who aren't afraid of governments and men who can, at worst, only kill them. Another safe, familiar context.

We also thank God for the United States of America, like ancient Israel recipient of God's blessing. We have no fear of death by execution or the lesser deaths of imprisonment, loss of educational opportunity for our children, an abrupt end to our careers.

There's no need for us to follow the martyrs' train. For other generations and other Christians today, suffering and death for their faith; for us, health and wealth.

So let's forget about those irrelevant words and get on with church growth, church building, and conferences on the inerrancy of the Bible.

But can we forget about them? Are inerrancy and irrelevancy really compatible? Can we relegate words of Jesus to the first century or twentieth century Russia?

If we believe that "All Scripture is given by inspiration of God" (2 Tim. 3:16, 17), can we deny that "all Scripture" is also "profitable for doctrine, for reproof, for correction, for instruction in righteousness"?

Future generations may well look upon our generation as the one that proved the Bible and considered the Bible irrelevant.

How can we obey Jesus' command not to fear men, because all they can do is kill the body? How obey it here in the United States today?

Perhaps there would be less passion in what I am writing if I did not include myself. I'm looking for answers to the question in my own comfortable life.

The first thing we see is that Jesus puts death in perspective. It's an enemy, but through His death and resurrection, it's a defeated enemy.

Don't let the fear that you may die keep you from taking risks, Jesus said. Death isn't the worst thing that could happen to you: God's judgment after death, his power to "Throw you into hell" (Luke 12:4–5 NIV) is the most terrible prospect a human could contemplate.

So be careless with your life.

During the great plagues that decimated Europe several centuries ago, Christians were careless with their lives. Knowing the awful consequences of contracting the disease, they accepted the responsibility to nurse victims and bury their bodies.

(It was out of such service during an early seventeenth century plague that Martin Rinkart wrote the great hymn, "Now Thank We All Our God." After his own wife and children died, Rinkart gave himself to caring for the sick and burying the dead.)

We don't have the bubonic plague in the United States, but we do have AIDS. Are we Christians distinguishing ourselves by risking exposure to the disease to provide care for its victims? If we are, I don't hear about it. Catholics are establishing centers and hospices; are Protestant evangelicals?

I haven't heard of Christians standing up for the right of AIDS-infected children to attend school.

We American Christians are worried about our health, as anxious to avoid dying as any of our contemporary worldlings, who, losing life, lose everything.

Do we seriously face the question of how much cost and care we should be given if we are dying and hope of recovery is gone?

I hear someone say, "Hope of recovery is never gone if you'll only trust God to heal." True, and so our most visible face to the world is that of the happy healer—not the compassionate friend who serves in a hospice. Our message is prolonged life in a fallen world, not eternal life in a perfect heaven.

Should Christians welcome heart transplants and other inordinately expensive procedures that extend life in this country, while infant and child mortality rates in the third world continue terribly high?

I remember when Christians were accused of living for "pie-in-the-sky." By 1954 a change had set in, and we were beginning to live for "pie-in-the-belly"—a term I used in my less-couth days as editor of *HIS* magazine. In that same thirty-two-year-ago editorial I wrote, "We must show non-Christians that the best earthly picnic cannot even be compared with a single day in the Father's house."

Last Sunday I saw an old friend, Herbert Kane. He has lived to serve Christ: first in China until the Communists put him out, later in teaching at Barrington College and Trinity Seminary. He's written a number of books.

Now he's retired in Oxford, Ohio. Retired? He's teaching students from Miami University who gather in his living room. He's speaking and traveling and writing books.

Fifteen years or so ago he was healed of cancer. (God does heal.) Now he continues to risk his life to serve Christ.

"To live is Christ, to die is gain" (Phil. 1:21)

# The Severity and Goodness of God

## September 1986

*Since I've shared the severity of God with my readers, I want to share the goodness of God in this final column.*

With the present issue, I complete twenty-five years of writing this column for *Eternity*. Since all things temporal come to an end, this is also the last column I shall write.

From my standpoint, the best result of this sort of writing, apart from the documentation of my opinions over a period of time, is the audience to whom I have had the privilege to speak. Often they talk back, sometimes through letters, other times when I meet them.

I was speaking on the West Coast about ten years ago when a brief incident occurred, which I prize. An elderly man came up to me afterward and said, as he shot out his hand, "I told the missus I had to come tonight because I already know you, but I wanted you to meet me."

On another occasion, a little farther south on the West coast, a woman told me that she had read my column for a number of years, then stated quite firmly, "I don't really think you are."

"You don't think I'm what?" I asked.

---

*Eternity* Editor's Note: Joe Bayly was chosen in 1961 as columnist a few months after the death of Dr. Donald Grey Barnhouse, *Eternity*'s founder. Although he had heavy responsibilities at David C. Cook Publishing Company, most recently as president, Joe enlivened the pages of *Eternity* for a quarter of a century.

Recently he decided to retire the column in favor of other writing commitments. This is his final column.

Then on July 16, 1986, after open-heart surgery, Joe went to be with the Lord. With love, we bid him farewell. —Russell T. Hitt, editor emeritus

"Out of your mind." Of course I thanked her for this affirmation, which others might not be willing to give.

Some readers know of the losses Mary Lou and I experienced around the time I began writing this column. (Over a six-year period three of our sons died, aged four years, three weeks, and eighteen years. Cause of death was different for each.) Our grief was reflected in certain columns.

The severity of God was evident in those crises. I couldn't hide it, although I felt then—and continue to feel—that this was more of a problem to some of our friends than to Mary Lou and me. We have found great comfort and peace in the sovereignty of God. And in the darkest hour we have not doubted His love.

Last week at Moody Bible Institute's pastors' conference, a man who had previously only known me through my writing asked, "I know you had three children die. What about the others who are still living?"

Since I've shared the severity of God, with my readers, I want to share the goodness of God in this final column, as I did with that pastor.

We have four children in addition to the three who died. I suppose we have had a heightened concept of our stewardship in raising them, being keenly aware that God could terminate our responsibility and call one of them home at any time.

Now they have all finished their training years, and, by God's grace, all are active in Christian ministry.

Deborah felt a strong call to work with inner-city kids.* After five years teaching in a public school on Chicago's West Side (an area that was burned out after Martin Luther King Jr.'s assassination), she has taught twelve years, and is now principal of Lake View Academy, a small alternative high school for a multi-ethnic group of students, many of whom have dropped out of public schools. The school is located in Lake View Presbyterian Church, a poor church that stayed put when many others moved to the suburbs or closed their doors.

---

*Deborah Bayly continues to serve as Principal of Lake View Academy, which celebrated its Twentieth Anniversary in October 1992.

I wish you could meet most of the kids who attend Lake View, as well as their graduates. The commitment of Deborah, Anita Smith (who founded the school), and the teaching staff—commitment to God and to their students—has had life-changing results.

Tim, our next oldest living child, is married to Mary Lee Taylor.* They have three children: Heather (nine), Joseph (four), and Michal (six months). Tim is beginning his fourth year of ministry at two Presbyterian churches in Wisconsin: Pardeeville (small town) and Rosedale (country). He is also active in the pro-life movement, serving on the board of Presbyterians Pro-Life. Tim and Mary Lee's door is always open to men and women in need.

Mary Lou and I recently gave Tim and Mary Lee a tenth anniversary present: a weekend at a Chicago hotel while we took care of their children and I preached for him. When I approached the pulpit in Pardeeville, I saw a small yellow "Post-it" on the preacher's side of the pulpit. Printed on it was "Dad, I love you."

David is our next child.* He graduated from seminary this spring. This past year he has had an invaluable experience as an intern at First Evangelical Free Church (where Chuck Swindoll is senior pastor) in Fullerton, California.

Two years ago David was a summer missionary with SEND in Glennallen, Alaska. In its different way, this was as valuable an experience as his more recent internship. Nurses at the small hospital and the couple who were responsible for the summer program made an indelible impression on him by their selfless service. A small Indian church also made a lasting impression.

Now David is waiting for God to lead him to the next step in his service.

---

*Tim and Mary Lee now have five children, Heather (sixteen), Joseph (eleven), Michal (seven), Hannah (four), and Taylor (one). Tim left his first pastorate in 1992 and currently serves as pastor of Evangelical Community Church in Bloomington, Indiana.

*David Bayly and his wife, Cheryl (McHenny) Bayly, have two children, Nathan (three) and Elizabeth (two). David has served as pastor of Springfield United Brethren Church in Monclova, Ohio, since 1988.

Nathan is our youngest.* His wife is Sandy Bennett. He also graduated from seminary in the spring and has become director of Christian education and youth ministry at Community Church in Bristol, Tennessee.

Sandy worked in an ophthalmologist's office and Nate painted houses (one built in 1691) to pay seminary expenses. One of Nate's best experiences was holding weekly Bible studies in a nursing home.

All our children are concerned for other people and involved in their lives, especially those who don't yet know Jesus Christ. The three who have homes demonstrate the gift of hospitality.

Mary Lou* and I are aware that all this represents the grace of God, but also that for ourselves and our children the road hasn't ended.

Yet we know that both by His severity and by His goodness God has shown consistent faithfulness. God is good. He is worthy of all trust and glory. Amen.

---

*Nathan and his wife, Sandy, live in Bristol, Tennessee, where Nathan has served as Pastor of Cornerstone Chapel since 1986.

Mary Lou Bayly ("Mud" to her children) continues to stay alive, happily, and to make her abode in the house where she and Joe shared many "winters" together. She loves to garden, to visit her children and grandchildren, to take part in neighborhood Bible studies, and one day a week she travels to Chicago to work with the students at Lake View Academy.

# INDEX